The BIG Book of
MOTIVATION
GAMES

Other books in *The Big Book of Business Games* series:

The Big Book of Business Games
The Big Book of Creativity Games (also by Robert Epstein)
The Big Book of Customer Service Training Games
The Big Book of Flip Charts
The Big Book of Humorous Training Games
The Big Book of Presentation Games
The Big Book of Sales Games
The Big Book of Stress-Relief Games (also by Robert Epstein)
The Big Book of Team Building Games

The BIG Book of

MOTIVATION
GAMES

Quick, Fun Activities
for Energizing People
at Work and at Home

Robert Epstein, Ph.D.

Editor-in-Chief, *Psychology Today*
University Research Professor, United States International University
Director Emeritus, Cambridge Center for Behavioral Studies
Chairman and CEO, InnoGen International

with **Jessica Rogers**
University of California Berkeley

McGraw-Hill

New York Chicago San Francisco
Lisbon London Madrid Mexico City
Milan New Delhi San Juan Seoul
Singapore Sydney Toronto

McGraw-Hill

A Division of The **McGraw·Hill** *Companies*

1 2 3 4 5 6 7 8 9 0   AGM / AGM   0 9 8 7 6 5 4 3 2 1 0

ISBN 0-07-137234-2

The sponsoring editor for this book was Richard Narramore, the editing supervisor was Sally Glover, and the production supervisor was Charles Annis. Printed and bound by QuebecorWorld / Martinsburg.

McGraw-Hill books are available at special quantity discounts to use as premiums and sales promotions, or for use in corporate training programs. For more information, please write to the Director of Special Sales, McGraw-Hill, 2 Penn Plaza, New York, NY 10121-2298. Or contact your local bookstore.

 This book is printed on recycled, acid-free paper containing a minimum of 50% recycled de-inked fiber.

To Jo Colman,
for the challenge.
(R. E.)

To Dad, for always asking,
Why isn't this A- an A+?
(J. R.)

CONTENTS

FIND THE RIGHT GAMES

Here's a quick guide for finding the game you need. Scan down until you find your purpose, then look up the games listed in that category. As you'll see, some games fit more than one category. The games are in alphabetical order by title—both here and in the body of the book—so you'll be able to locate the actual game using just the title (page numbers are included, as well). The detailed index in the back of the book will also help you find the game you need.

GAMES FOR MOTIVATING YOURSELF

Purpose: *Perform at Your Peak*
Games:
Aiming for Actualization (p. 23)
All That You Can Be (p. 29)
The Bliss List (Individ. Ver.) (p. 47)
The Color of Motivation (p. 61)
The Crystal Ball Game (p. 69)
Higher and Higher (p. 115)
The I-Do Game (p. 119)
Ergonometry (p. 83)
I Have a Dream (p. 123)
Keeping the Fires Burning (p. 129)

King of the Hill (p. 135)
The Midas Touch (p. 141)
The Mover-Shaker Game (p. 149)
The Slump Game (p. 161)
The Star Chart Game (p. 169)
Target Practice (p. 177)
The Ten-Year Plan (p. 184)
The Twenty-Eight-Hour Day (p. 197)
What D'Ya Know? (Individ. Ver.) (p. 201)

Purpose: *Stop Procrastinating*
Games:
Beat the Clock! (p. 45)
Blowing Away the Tension (p. 53)
The Crystal Ball Game (p. 69)
Goal-a-Rama I (p. 91)
The I-Do Game (p. 119)

I Have a Dream (p. 123)
Keeping the Fires Burning (p. 129)
The Mover-Shaker Game (p. 149)
The Star Chart Game (p. 169)
The Twenty-Eight-Hour Day (p. 197)

Purpose: *Boost Your Energy When It's Low*
Games:
All That You Can Be (p. 29)
The Bliss List (Individ. Ver.) (p. 47)
The Color of Motivation (p. 61)
The Crystal Ball Game (p. 69)
Feed Me! (p. 87)
Goal-a-Rama I (p. 91)
The Goodfellas Game (p. 107)

Higher and Higher (p. 115)
The I-Do Game (p. 119)
King of the Hill (p. 135)
Make Me Laugh (p. 139)
The Midas Touch (p. 141)
The Mover-Shaker Game (p. 149)
The Slump Game (p. 161)

Purpose: *Feel Less Overwhelmed*
Games:
Beat the Clock! (p. 45)
The Bliss List (Individ. Ver.) (p. 47)
Blowing Away the Tension (p. 53)

The Goodfellas Game (p. 107)
Make Me Laugh (p. 139)
The Mover-Shaker Game (p. 149)

GAMES FOR MOTIVATING YOUR TEAM

xiv

Purpose: **_Motivate Chronically Underperforming Employees_**

Games:

Aiming for Actualization (p. 23)	Higher and Higher (p. 115)
All That You Can Be (p. 29)	The I-Do Game (p. 119)
The Bliss List (Individ. Ver.) (p. 47)	I Have a Dream (p. 123)
Anonymous Suggestion Game (p. 39)	Keeping the Fires Burning (p. 129)
The Bliss List (Individ. Ver.) (p. 47)	King of the Hill (p. 135)
Blowing Away the Tension (p. 53)	The Midas Touch (p. 141)
The Careful Critique Game (p. 57)	The Mover-Shaker Game (p. 149)
The Crystal Ball Game (p. 69)	The Slump Game (p. 161)
Feed Me! (p. 87)	The Star Chart Game (p. 169)
Goal-a-Rama I (p. 91)	Target Practice (p. 177)
Goal-a-Rama II (p. 95)	The Tchotchke Game (p. 181)
Goal-a-Rama III (p. 99)	The Ten-Year Plan (p. 184)
Goal-a-Rama IV (p. 101)	Workplace Challenge (p. 213)
The Goodfellas Game (p. 107)	

Purpose: **_Spark Peak Team Performance_**

Games:

All That You Can Be (p. 29)	Goal-a-Rama IV (p. 101)
The A-Mazing Maze Game (p. 33)	Group vs. Team (p. 111)
The Bliss List (Team Version) (p. 51)	Higher and Higher (p. 115)
The Careful Critique Game (p. 57)	The I-Do Game (p. 119)
The Color of Motivation (p. 61)	I Have a Dream (p. 123)
Crossing That Bridge (p. 65)	King of the Hill (p. 135)
The Dream Team (p. 79)	The Midas Touch (p. 141)
Feed Me! (p. 87)	The Star Chart Game (p. 169)
Goal-a-Rama I (p. 91)	The Tchotchke Game (p. 181)
Goal-a-Rama II (p. 95)	The Yes! Game (p. 217)
Goal-a-Rama III (p. 99)	

Purpose: **_Help a Team Set and Meet Goals_**

Games:

Anonymous Suggestion Game (p. 39)	The Dream Team (p. 79)
Beat the Clock! (p. 45)	Goal-a-Rama I (p. 91)
The Bliss List (Team Version) (p. 51)	Goal-a-Rama II (p. 95)
The Careful Critique Game (p. 57)	Goal-a-Rama III (p. 99)
The Color of Motivation (p. 61)	Goal-a-Rama IV (p. 101)
Crossing That Bridge (p. 65)	Group vs. Team (p. 111)
The Crystal Ball Game (p. 69)	I Have a Dream (p. 123)

Purpose: **_Motivate People in a Large Organization_**

Games:

Aiming for Actualization (p. 23)	Goal-a-Rama III (p. 99)
All That You Can Be (p. 29)	Goal-a-Rama IV (p. 101)
Anonymous Suggestion Game (p. 39)	The Goodfellas Game (p. 107)
The Bliss List (Individ. Ver.) (p. 47)	Group vs. Team (p. 111)
The Bliss List (Team Ver.) (p. 51)	Higher and Higher (p. 115)
The Careful Critique Game (p. 57)	The I-Do Game (p. 119)
The Color of Motivation (p. 61)	I Have a Dream (p. 123)
Crossing That Bridge (p. 65)	Keeping the Fires Burning (p. 129)
The Crystal Ball Game (p. 69)	King of the Hill (p. 135)
Ergonometry (p. 83)	The Midas Touch (p. 141)
Feed Me! (p. 87)	The Mover-Shaker Game (p. 152)
Goal-a-Rama I (p. 91)	The Star Chart Game (p. 169)
Goal-a-Rama II (p. 95)	The Tchotchke Game (p. 181)

Purpose:	**_Use Competition as a Motivational Tool_**	
Games:	The A-Mazing Maze Game (p. 33)	Goal-a-Rama I (p. 91)
	Beat the Clock! (p. 45)	Group vs. Team (p. 111)
	Crossing That Bridge (p. 65)	The No-Hands Game (p. 153)
	Feed Me! (p. 87)	

GAMES FOR A WORKSHOP

Purpose:	**_Games for a Half-Day Motivation Workshop_**	
Games:	All That You Can Be (p. 29)	Goal-a-Rama I (p. 91)
	What D'Ya Know? (Individ. Ver.) (p. 201)	The Mover-Shaker Game (p. 149)
	The Yes! Game (p. 217)	The Goodfellas Game (p. 107)
	Different Strokes (p. 73)	Group vs. Team (p. 111)
	Feed Me! (p. 87)	Workplace Challenge (p. 213)
	The Bliss List (Individ. Ver.) (p. 47)	King of the Hill (p. 135)

ACKNOWLEDGMENTS

We're grateful to our editor at McGraw-Hill, Richard Narramore, for motivating us with money and praise. When he wasn't available, we relied on donuts from VG's (Cardiff by the Sea, California), brownies from Henry's Marketplace (Encinitas, California), and bagels from the Cardiff Seaside Market. We owe special thanks to the McDonald's in Encinitas for freshly baked chocolate chip cookies, without which half the chapters in this book might not exist.

The BIG Book of

MOTIVATION

GAMES

getting

ready...

MOTIVATION BASICS

I knew an administrator once—let's call her Ann—who confessed to me that she hated her job so much that she had trouble making the trip to work in the morning. Sometimes, she said, she stopped halfway, pulled over, and had long debates with herself about turning back. On all but a few occasions, she eventually made it to work—where she struggled to keep up appearances and get things done. Ann had suffered through this regimen for years, at first counting the months, then the weeks, then the days that would bring her to retirement.

Ann was living half a life, her staff was getting half a supervisor and was probably performing at half steam, and her organization was getting half an employee—a poor arrangement all around.

Then again, at least she was getting to the office. Some people don't make it.

When your energy is low, what, if anything, can you do about it? If your employees are sluggish, how can you give them a boost?

Researchers in business, psychology, and other fields have been working hard (speaking of motivation) for decades to answer these questions, and significant advances have been made.

If you or your staff are only going through the motions—if *passion* and *energy* are only words you see in Nike ads—get ready for liftoff.

What Is Motivation?

Motivation is an internal state of arousal that often precedes behavior. As Ann's case teaches us, the relationship between motivation and behavior is only approximate: One can behave without being motivated to behave. One can also be motivated to behave—for example, to date an attractive colleague—without ever having an opportunity to behave.

Ideally, we not only experience a high state of arousal, but we also have an opportunity to behave in a way that fulfills our need. When we're hungry, for example, we feel great if we can eat. When we're edgy, we feel frustrated if we're prevented from moving around.

If you're already highly motivated and can't find a way to reach your goals, you might want to read books on creativity, career change, or—if all else fails—stress management. This book focuses on the opposite problem—the lack of motivation, either in yourself or in those around you. How can you induce an internal state of arousal? In other words, how can you make yourself or others *want* to behave? How can you get people to *strive* to achieve? To *yearn* to reach goals?

These are important questions, because if behavior and motivation aren't in sync—if people are just dragging themselves through the day or if they lack the opportunity to act on some impulse—performance, productivity, mood, health, and retention all suffer.

What are the key factors that produce that *wanting*?

Factors

Motivation is generated by a variety of factors, some of which we can control, and some of which we can't. We're stuck with our genes, for example, and our genetic makeup constrains how we react to the world. Some people are naturally energetic; others more reserved.

We also can't control our "environmental histories"—the set of experiences we've had up until the present moment. We didn't pick our parents, the neighborhoods in which we were raised, the economy of our country, the items in the headlines, and so on.

But from this moment on, there are at least 13 factors (also called "variables") that we can manipulate to some extent to boost our motivation:

> *Exercise:* Physical activity, especially aerobic activity, tends to boost energy.
>
> *Good nutrition:* Some foods make us sluggish, and others make us energetic. Books like *Food and Mood*, by Elizabeth Somer, can help us plan energizing diets. Nutritional supplements, taken wisely, can also assist.
>
> *Sleep:* Lack of sleep is probably the most common reason for poor motivation. Even if rewards are at hand, it's hard to recognize them if you're tired.
>
> *Rewards:* We can give rewards of various sorts to other people (awards, respect, money, praise, recognition, promotions, raises, vacations, time off, and so on), and we can also put ourselves in rewarding

situations. We can help develop incentive programs for our companies; we can seek jobs with better incentive systems; we can seek out kinder, more generous friends.

Challenges: Some people are motivated by challenges; other are scared of them. Seek challenge, avoid challenge, or arrange challenges for others, as appropriate.

Friendship: Many of us will work for low pay if we get to work with great people. Companionship and camaraderie produce that great feeling of *wanting*. Alas, personality conflicts have just the opposite effect. Find the right people with whom to work and play. Take personal characteristics into account when assembling teams.

Kindness: Some people will do anything for a kind word and some decent treatment. If kindness is important to you, seek it out. If kindness is important to your staff members, develop a kind streak.

Security: Most people want to feel safe and secure, and they want to feel that their futures are safe and secure. If security is important to you, find a job or career that provides it. If an outstanding employee wants more security, provide stock options or a long-term contract.

Authority: A few people are highly motivated by power. If power's your trip, find or create a position that gives you authority. If an employee is turned on by power, try giving him or her more authority.

Independence: Some of us value autonomy, ownership, and independence above everything else. Self-employment might be the key.

Pleasant environment: Many people need the colors, sounds, and textures of the workplace to feel right. If the right chair is important for you, save up and buy it. If your employees keep moaning about the hum from flourescent lights, replace them.

Creative expression: If you're burning with a desire to express yourself, find a job or career that lets you do that, and then set up an easel at home. If your staff members are brooding because their new ideas don't seem welcome, upgrade your management skills.

Meaning: For some, the quest for meaning is the greatest motivator of all. If, for you, it's meaning over money, find a job you in which you can believe. If your employees are losing faith, you might be able to add more meaning to their lives by clarifying the vision of your organization.

The figure on page 12 can help you present these factors to a group. When thinking about factors that affect motivation, also keep two critical considerations in mind:

The Different-Strokes Principle:
What motivates one person might not motivate another.

The Things-Change Principle:
What motivates someone one day might not work the next.

You can use the overhead on page 13 to help present these ideas.

Skill, Not Will

If you're trying to boost your motivation, can't you just bear down, concentrate, and *will* yourself to be motivated? Some TV gurus would have you believe that this is possible, but "will power" works poorly for most people. Our motto is "Skill, Not Will," by which we mean that the best way to change oneself and one's future is to learn and practice new skills. Skill acquisition has a number of advantages over will power. For one thing, it saves you a good deal of grunting and groaning. Second, it prepares you for the long term; gathering up your courage might get you through the next few minutes, but it's hard to count on in the long term. Third, the right set of skills will help you deal with changing conditions—a new boss, an aging body, or a fluctuating economy.

Eight different types of skills—also called "competencies"—can help you build and maintain high motivation. The skilled individual:

1) *Manages the environment:* You create a workspace that helps to energize you, and you surround yourself with people who bring out your best.

2) *Manages thoughts:* You use visualization techniques, thought-restructuring techniques, and affirmations to keep yourself thinking positively.

3) *Sets goals:* You make both short-term and long-term goals, and you formulate plans for how to achieve those goals.

4) *Maintains a healthful lifestyle:* You exercise regularly, get adequate sleep, and eat right in order to keep your energy high.

5) *Makes commitments:* You make commitments to yourself and to others in order to arrange both positive and negative consequences for your behavior.

6) *Monitors behavior:* You keep records of your progress in order to bring yourself closer to your goals.

7) *Manages stress:* You practice relaxation techniques, reduce sources of stress in your environment, and plan ahead in order to stay calm and productive.

8) *Manages rewards:* You seek out people who appreciate you and settings that reward you.

The first four of these competencies can be measured using the *Epstein Motivation Competencies Inventory for Individuals (EMCI-i)*, an abridged form of which is included near the end of this book (see page 205). All of the competencies are listed on the overhead on page 14.

Managers, supervisors, parents, and teachers need a slightly different set of competencies—10 in all—to motivate other people. The skilled manager:

1) *Manages rewards:* You provide positive and constructive feedback, recognize achievement, and reward good performance.

2) *Communicates effectively:* You solicit ideas and feedback, present a clear vision of the future, and seek to inform, educate, and inspire.

3) *Manages teams effectively:* You compose teams wisely and help them to function smoothly and optimally.

4) *Manages the environment:* You create and maintain an attractive, functional workspace and encourage healthy relationships.

5) *Matches skills and tasks:* You match people's skills with the tasks they're assigned.

6) *Challenges:* You identify people who thrive on challenge, and you seek to push them beyond their current limits.

7) *Trains:* You identify current skill levels and provide ongoing training to enhance a wide variety of skills.

8) *Resolves conflicts:* You identify conflicts and resolve them before they escalate.

9) *Allocates resources wisely:* You allocate resources in ways that people perceive as both generous and fair.

10) *Models high motivation:* You demonstrate high energy, commitment, and enthusiasm in your work.

The first four of these competencies can be measured using a second test, the *Epstein Motivation Competencies Inventory for Managers (EMCI-m)*, an abridged version of which is also included in this book (see page 211). All 10 are listed in the overhead on page 15, and the overhead on page 16 lists some common rewards that are useful in the business environment. Books like Bob Nelson's *1001 Ways To Energize Employees* can give you many other ideas for structuring reward programs.

Want More?

The full version of the *EMCI-i* and the *EMCI-m* can be obtained from InnoGen International (1-800-INNOGEN or www.innogen.com). If you just need a pep talk, contact Dr. Epstein at repstein@post.harvard.edu. Constructive feedback (see "The Careful Critique Game," page 57) is always welcome.

FACTORS UNDERLYING MOTIVATION

- ✴ Exercise
- ✴ Good Nutrition
- ✴ Sleep
- ✴ Rewards
- ✴ Challenges
- ✴ Friendship
- ✴ Kindness
- ✴ Security
- ✴ Authority
- ✴ Independence
- ✴ Pleasant Environment
- ✴ Creative Expression
- ✴ Meaning

KEY MOTIVATIONAL PRINCIPLES

✳ **THE <u>DIFFERENT-STROKES</u> PRINCIPLE:**

What motivates one person
might not motivate another.

✳ **THE <u>THINGS-CHANGE</u> PRINCIPLE:**

What motivates someone one day
might not work the next.

COMPETENCIES NEEDED TO
BOOST INDIVIDUAL MOTIVATION

❶ MANAGES THE ENVIRONMENT
❷ MANAGES THOUGHTS
❸ SETS GOALS
❹ MAINTAINS A HEALTHFUL LIFESTYLE
❺ MAKES COMMITMENTS
❻ MONITORS BEHAVIOR
❼ MANAGES STRESS
❽ MANAGES REWARDS

Competencies Managers Need To Motivate Others

❶ Manages Rewards
❷ Communicates Effectively
❸ Manages Teams Effectively
❹ Manages the Environment
❺ Matches Skills and Tasks
❻ Challenges
❼ Trains
❽ Resolves Conflicts
❾ Allocates Resources Wisely
❿ Models High Motivation

REWARDS PEOPLE LOVE!

➢ Tickets for Sporting Event
➢ *Food!*
➢ Dinner at Favorite Restaurant
➢ *Money!*
➢ Recognition
➢ Promotion

➢ Time Off
➢ Improved Work Environment
➢ *A Raise!*
➢ Movie Tickets
➢ Increased Work Area Space

➢ Book by Favorite Author
➢ Praise
➢ Equity
➢ Awards
➢ Discounts
➢ Special Privileges

MAKING THE MOST OF THIS BOOK

We're here to motivate you, so this book is structured to keep you moving. Each game chapter gives you a "nutshell" synopsis of the game, tells you how the game can be used, how long the game takes to play, and what kinds of material and supplies you'll need to play. You're then given instructions for playing the game, some discussion questions, and various alternatives and tips for customizing the game.

We've given you several easy ways to find the games that suit your needs: First, you can check the "Find the Right Games" section that follows the table of contents at the beginning of this book. Find your application, then look up the games listed below each application. For example, if you're looking for games to fight procrastination, look at the list under that heading on page xiii. Then look up games like "Beat the Clock!" and "The Twenty-Eight-Hour Day" to see if they suit your needs.

The games themselves are in alphabetical order by title, so once you're familiar with some of the (awesome!) titles, you'll be able to find your favorite games easily. You can also locate games by using the detailed index at the end of the book.

If you're looking for a few good games for a half-day seminar on motivation, check out the list we've provided on page xviii. The overheads in the previous chapter, "Motivation Basics," can be used to help you introduce the concept of motivation.

If time allows, we suggest you begin your seminar with one of the "motivation competency" tests included in the "What D'Ya Know?" chapters (pages 201 and 207). The first test, the *EMCI-i* (page 201), is for individuals seeking to boost their own motivation, and the second test, the *EMCI-m* (page 207), is for managers, teachers, supervisors, and parents seeking to boost motivation in others. The tests will help you discover where people's skills are weak, and you can then select games to strengthen particular skills.

Here are some basic competency areas—the ones tested in the abridged tests included in this book—along with games that can help you build those competencies:

INDIVIDUAL Competency 1
Manages the Environment
Games: The Bliss List (Individual Version) (p. 47)
              The Color of Motivation (p. 61)
              Ergonometry (p. 83)
              Keeping the Fires Burning (p. 129)
              Stacked to the Ceiling (p. 165)
              Target Practice (p. 177)

INDIVIDUAL Competency 2
Manages Thoughts
Games: Aiming for Actualization (p. 23)
              All That You Can Be (p. 29)
              The Crystal Ball Game (p. 69)
              King of the Hill (p. 135)
              Make Me Laugh (p. 139)
              The Midas Touch (p. 141)

INDIVIDUAL Competency 3
Sets Goals
Games: Aiming for Actualization (p. 23)
              Goal-a-Rama I (p. 91)

<u>*MANAGERIAL Competency 3*</u>
Manages Teams Effectively

Games: The Bliss List (Team Version) (p. 51)
Crossing That Bridge (p. 65)
The Dream Team (p. 79)
Goal-a-Rama II (p. 95)
Goal-a-Rama III (p. 99)
Goal-a-Rama IV (p. 101)
Group vs. Team (p. 111)
Thinking Caps (p. 189)

<u>*MANAGERIAL Competency 4*</u>
Manages the Environment

Games: The Color of Motivation (p. 61)
Ergonometry (p. 83)
Workplace Challenge (p. 213)

Whether you use a competencies approach, an applications approach (see "Find the Right Games," page xiii), or you just pick and choose your games to have some fun, we hope this collection will energize and entertain both you and your colleagues. If you have to drag yourself out of bed in the morning, if your hopes and dreams are distant memories, if the drive to work in the morning is painful, then Blow Away the Tension, Aim for Actualization, practice The Midas Touch, make a Ten-Year Plan, and—well, just keep reading!

the
games!

AIMING FOR ACTUALIZATION

In a Nutshell

Participants identify some of their most
basic needs and devise strategies for meeting them.

What It's For

Use this game if you want to: perform at your peak; envision
and achieve your personal goals; fight boredom; motivate
your staff members to perform at their peak; improve your
managerial skills; help people through tough times; motivate
chronically underperforming employees; motivate people in a
large organization.

Time

15–20 minutes.

What You'll Learn

Motivation arises from attempts to meet one's needs.

What You'll Need

Writing materials should be provided for all participants. You may wish to distribute copies of the handout on page 26 or of the overhead on page 27.

What to Do

Briefly review Abraham Maslow's *hierarchy of needs*, perhaps from a list you display on an overhead (see page 27). Maslow, a humanistic psychologist, believed that people have an innate order of needs that determine their actions. These begin with the most basic physiological needs (like food, clothing, and shelter), without which, presumably, "higher" needs could not be addressed. Once the most basic needs are met, "safety" needs can be attended to; once these are met, "social" needs can be attended to, and so on. At the top of the pyramid is the need for "self-actualization," an almost Zen-like state of fulfillment and self-satisfaction. In an affluent society—especially among successful professionals—self-actualization has long held great fascination.

Ask participants to complete each level of a "personal pyramid," as follows: For each of the five levels, have them estimate the percentage of need that they've currently fulfilled. Then have them state, for each level, what they're missing. Finally, ask them to devise a strategy for meeting their needs more fully at each level.

Call on volunteers to discuss their plans, and lead a discussion about the results.

Discussion Questions

1. Which of your needs have you met? Which have you not met?
2. How might fulfillment strategies help you meet needs you haven't met?
3. What strategies might help you meet those needs?
4. Why is it important to understand our needs?

Alternative

You can expand the game with more elaborate written materials. For example, divide each of the five levels into three parts: Percentage Completed, Unfulfilled Needs, and Fulfillment Strategy. Tally the percentages in each category and display the results for the group. Look for common unfulfilled needs, and facilitate a discussion in which people search for fulfillment strategies.

If You're Short on Time

Briefly review Maslow's hierarchy of needs. Then display the pyramid on an overhead, and discuss fulfillment strategies with the group.

Your Personal Pyramid

Complete each section below

SELF-ACTUALIZATION
Percentage complete:
Fulfillment strategy:

SELF-ESTEEM
Percentage complete:
Fulfillment strategy:

SOCIAL CONTACT
Percentage complete:
Fulfillment strategy:

SAFETY
Percentage complete:
Fulfillment strategy:

FOOD & SHELTER
Percentage complete:
Fulfillment strategy:

Pyramid of Needs

Self-Actualization
The desire for self-fulfillment; becoming
everything one is capable of becoming.

Self-Esteem
The need for a stable, high level of self-respect;
the need for respect from others in order to feel satisfied
and valuable. If these needs are not met, we sometimes
feel inferior or worthless.

Social Contact
The need to escape loneliness and alienation
and to experience love, affection, and a sense of belonging.

Safety
The need for security.

Food & Shelter
Basic biological needs such as food, water, and shelter.

ALL THAT
YOU CAN BE

In a Nutshell

In a partially-guided imagery exercise, participants visualize themselves working at their peak performance.

What It's For

Use this game if you want to: perform at your peak; boost your energy when it's low; envision and achieve your personal goals; motivate your staff members to perform at their peak; motivate chronically underperforming employees; spark peak team performance; motivate people in a large organization; motivate salespeople.

Time

10 minutes.

What You'll Learn

Performance you never imagined yourself achieving can at least be imagined!

What You'll Need

No special materials are needed.

What to Do

Advise participants to sit in a relaxed position, close their eyes, and breathe easily. Then recite the following text in a soothing voice:

> *Continue to breathe easily and clear your minds. Listen very closely to my voice. Focus on the sound of my voice and feel your body relax. Listen carefully to my instructions, and continue to breathe easily.... With your eyes closed and your body relaxed, I want you to envision a work situation—one which is very important to you. It's a situation in which you're not currently performing at your peak.... Around you now an image of this work situation is slowly starting to form. I want you to become aware of all the details of this scene.... Look around.... What does the room look like? Are there other people around? Gradually, let your image grow clearer.... Look around again, slowly.... What time of day is it? What sounds do you hear?*
>
> *Now shift your focus onto yourself. Envision yourself performing in that situation. Picture yourself performing in an exemplary way—the very, very best performance you can possibly image—a performance that is extraordinary, even super-human.... Now let yourself imagine the outcomes of your performance.... How will*

others react? Envision rewards or compensation for your super-human performance.... What positive outcomes can you envision in the near future? In the distant future?

Let's go back to your original situation.... Once again, envision yourself performing in this outstanding way. Gradually, examine the details of your performance .... Pay attention to your emotional state.... How do you feel? Concentrate on the tone of your voice.... How is your body positioned? Notice how you're using your hands.... Let yourself feel a sense of exhilaration as you complete the performance. Let a sense of pride and self-worth fill you completely, knowing the wonderful consequences that will follow, knowing how extraordinary your performance has been.... Gradually, slowly, holding onto that feeling of exhilaration, open your eyes.

Next, ask some volunteers to report to the group about what their super-human performance was like.

Discussion Questions

1.   Did the feeling of pride and exhilaration persist after I asked you to open your eyes? How do you feel right now?
2.   How might you use this technique in the workplace? At home?
3.   Could you call up this image in the future? Will you need a tape, or could you visualize this on your own?

4.   What qualities of your super-human character could be transferred to your real character?

Alternative

As time allows, repeat this game with other work situations, or with personal situations, such as performance in bowling, golf, or baseball.

Tip!

Be sure to keep your voice quiet and soothing as you guide participants through their visualization. Distracting noises can be a bother for some people, so you might want to close doors and windows before you begin.

Personal Touch

Put the image text on tape for yourself, perhaps with some soothing background music. Just press and play!

THE A-MAZING
MAZE GAME

In a Nutshell

Volunteers race through a maze competition.

What It's For

Use this game if you want to: motivate your staff members to perform at their peak; spark peak team performance; use competition as a motivational tool.

Time

15 minutes.

What You'll Learn

Competition can help you achieve your goals.

What You'll Need

You'll need three stopwatches, three chairs, and two small tables. You'll also need three pencils (with erasers) and two mazes of approximately equal difficulty. The mazes on pages 37 and 38 should suffice, but be advised that they're probably too easy for some audiences. If you need special mazes to suit your needs, you can generate them for free at a Website created by John Lauro of the University of Michigan (www.flint.umich.edu/Departments/ITS/crac/maze.form.html).

What to Do

Part One: Appoint three participants as Mazemakers #1, #2, and #3, and also appoint three Timekeepers. Seat the Mazemakers so that #1 and #2 are at a small table on one side of the room and #3 is at a table on the other side of the room. Inform Mazemakers #1 and #2 that they're competing against each other, while #3 is completing the maze on his or her own.

Assign a Timekeeper to each Mazemaker; however, the Timekeepers should not be near the Mazemakers during the competition. Give a pencil to each Mazemaker and a stopwatch, ready to go, to each Timekeeper. Make sure the Timekeepers know which button to press to start and stop timing! (All of the timing can also be done on wristwatches, if you want to keep things simple.)

Now distribute copies of the first maze to each of the Mazemakers, and explain the goal of the maze task: to draw a continuous line from the entry point to the exit point in the maze. Each is marked with an arrow. Instruct the Mazemakers to begin the task on your signal and to raise their hands high when they're done. On your "Go!" signal, have the three Timekeepers keep track of their respective Mazemaker's performance. When all three Mazemakers are

34

done, record the completion times on a blackboard or flipchart.

Part Two: The task is the same; however, this time Mazemaker #2 moves over to #3's table. In other words, he or she is now competing with #3, and #1 is on his or her own. Distribute copies of the second maze to your three Mazemakers, and repeat the task.

When the second competition is over, put the completion times on the board, and lead a brief discussion about the effect that direct competition had on the outcomes of the two tasks.

Discussion Questions

1.   Did the Mazemakers perform differently in these two tasks? How so? Why?
2.   How does this game demonstrate the importance of competition?
3.   Why does competition increase motivation?
4.   What are some advantages of competition? What are some disadvantages?

Tip!

In a paper published in 1898 (yes, that's 1898, not 1998), psychologist Norman Triplett demonstrated that bicyclists ride faster when they have companions than when they ride alone. Although competition can be strenuous and sometimes even harmful, it generally improves performance. By the way, individual variation can skew the results in this game, so try to pick Mazemakers of roughly equal ability.

A-MAZING MAZE #1!

A-MAZING MAZE #2!

THE ANONYMOUS SUGGESTION GAME

In a Nutshell

Participants make suggestions for solving a sensitive societal problem—either with or without the protection of anonymity.

What It's For

Use this game if you want to: motivate your staff members to perform at their peak; motivate chronically underperforming employees; help a team set and meet goals; motivate people in a large organization; jump-start your creativity.

Time

15–20 minutes.

What You'll Learn

People are usually more motivated to express their creative ideas when they can do so anonymously—that is, when the risk of ridicule or punishment is removed.

What You'll Need

You'll need to create two different survey forms—those that protect anonymity and those that don't. You may want to use copies of the forms on pages 43 and 44.

What to Do

Distribute Form 1 (page 43) to half the group and Form 2 (page 44) to the other half. Explain that you're going to be comparing the types of suggestions people make when they must reveal their identities to the types of suggestions they make when they can remain anonymous. (In fact, that's not exactly what this game is about. We'll get to that in a minute.)

Have people list suggestions for reducing crime on our nation's streets. You can propose a different task if you like. Make it relevant to your particular group.

After the forms have been completed, explain that you're not actually interested in comparing the types of suggestions that have been made but rather the *number* of suggestions. Do people make more suggestions—especially on sensitive topics—when their identities are secret?

Have a volunteer collect the forms and compile a quick tally of the number of suggestions made by members of each half of the group. If the group is typical, people in the anonymous half will have made many more suggestions (on the average) than people in the half without anonymity. (In a small group, outlying values can unfairly skew the mean; the more appropriate statistic is the median.)

Lead a discussion about how these results can be applied to improve suggestion systems in the participants' work environments. What is the ideal suggestion system for motivating people to express their creative ideas on a regular basis? (See "Tips!" that follow for suggestions.)

Discussion Questions

1. Do people respond differently when their anonymity is assured? How so?
2. Even assuming that people are more honest or creative when they can remain anonymous, a suggestion system that does not allow people to claim their good ideas would surely fail. Why?
3. What's wrong with a suggestion system that requires people to identify themselves?
4. Why are people often reluctant to contribute their ideas to the group?

Tips!

In the workplace, you can boost creative expression by establishing a suggestion system that promotes capturing: an anonymous suggestion system that allows people to claim their ideas later. How you set this up—with two-part numbered suggestion forms, with special email addresses and codes, with a bulletin board system—depends on your particular work environment.

Remember, a new idea is like a gold brick falling from the sky: Everyone wants to catch it, but no one wants to be crushed by it. And all but a few think that it's probably fool's gold, anyway.

Survey (Form 1)
The Anonymous Suggestion Game

Your name (required):_____ Telephone (required):_____

Other contact information:_____

Please list your suggestions below:_____

1.

2.

3.

4.

5.

6.

7.

8.

9.

10.

Survey (Form 2)
The Anonymous Suggestion Game

Please list your suggestions below:

1.

2.

3.

4.

5.

6.

7.

8.

9.

10.

BEAT THE CLOCK!

In a Nutshell

Volunteers build card houses in this race against the clock.

What It's For

Use this game if you want to: stop procrastinating; feel less overwhelmed; help others to stop procrastinating; help a team set and meet goals; motivate salespeople; jump-start your creativity; manage your stress; use competition as a motivational tool.

Time

20 minutes.

What You'll Learn

Structure counts.

What You'll Need

You'll need lots of standard playing cards—at least 26 cards per person (half a deck). You'll also need a timer, a ruler, and a floor or other surface suitable for building card houses.

What to Do

Divide the group into small teams, and have the teams build the highest card house they can in the time allotted. In a 15-minute session, at least a few houses should reach 6 inches or higher.

Lead a brief discussion about the importance of being organized, working methodically, and building a strong foundation for any structure.

Discussion Questions

1. How could the results of this game be applied to your workplace?
2. What method or methods did you use to create the card house? How did you manage your time?
3. Why is time management important in achieving your goals?

Alternative

You can alter the time allotted or the number of cards provided, and you can also use other building materials: toothpicks, popsicle sticks, sugar cubes, or even business cards. A great alternative is to use regular letter-size sheets of paper, giving about 100 sheets to each person or team. It can take some real creativity to fold paper into shapes that will generate some height.

If You're Short on Time

Allow only 5 or 10 minutes for the construction!

THE BLISS LIST
(INDIVIDUAL VERSION)

In a Nutshell

Participants create and post their own lists of enjoyable activities to make it more likely that they'll engage in such activities during the day.

What It's For

Use this game if you want to: perform at your peak; boost your energy when it's low; feel less overwhelmed; envision and achieve your personal goals; fight boredom; motivate your staff members to perform at their peak; improve your managerial skills; help people through tough times; motivate chronically underperforming employees; motivate people in a large organization; motivate salespeople; manage your stress; design a motivating environment.

Time

15–20 minutes.

What You'll Learn

The motivating power of the Bliss List!

What You'll Need

Writing materials and a flipchart or blackboard.

What to Do

Remind participants that we often let days or weeks or even months go by without doing any of the simple things that make us feel our best. Tell them that one simple way to fight this tendency is to create and post a Bliss List—a list of activities that make you feel great.

Have participants spend a few minutes listing as many enjoyable activities as they can.

Finally, ask people to make a written commitment to post copies of their Bliss Lists in at least three specific places:

> *I hereby commit to posting copies of my Bliss List in all of the places I've listed above, with the intention of reminding myself to engage in as many of the listed activities as possible, as often as possible.*

_____

Signature

Discussion Questions

1.   Bliss Lists need to be updated from time to time. Why?

2.   How can you make it more likely that you'll keep your Bliss List up-to-date?

3.   Why is it important that Bliss Lists be posted and not simply written down?

4.   How could you use your computer to post your Bliss List?

THE BLISS LIST (TEAM VERSION)

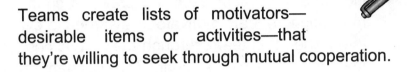

In a Nutshell

Teams create lists of motivators—
desirable items or activities—that
they're willing to seek through mutual cooperation.

What It's For

Use this game if you want to: fight boredom; improve your
managerial skills; spark peak team performance; help a team
set and meet goals; motivate people in a large organization;
motivate salespeople; manage your stress; design a
motivating environment.

Time

15–20 minutes.

What You'll Learn

Identifying team motivators can boost team spirit and improve
performance.

What You'll Need

Writing materials and a flipchart or blackboard.

What to Do

First, lead a brief discussion about the difference between individual motivation (see the previous chapter) and team motivation. A team motivator is awarded to everyone on the team when that team, through the mutual cooperation of its members, reaches a goal. The pennant awarded to a baseball team is an example of such a motivator. Sometimes managers may choose rewards for team performance without first determining the appeal of those rewards. When teams choose their rewards, motivation and performance improves.

Divide participants up into teams, and have the teams spend a few minutes listing as many rewards as they can—rewards the entire group is willing to work for—the Team Bliss List.

Finally, have people devise ways the Team Bliss List can be applied, posted, and kept up-to-date.

Discussion Questions

1. Bliss lists need to be updated as time goes by. Why?
2. How do team motivators differ from individual motivators?
3. Why is it important that Team Bliss Lists be distributed and posted?

BLOWING AWAY
THE TENSION

In a Nutshell

Participants learn the "cleansing breath" and are taught ways they might use it during the day to stay on track.

What It's For

Use this game if you want to: stop procrastinating; feel less overwhelmed; overcome anxiety and the fear of failure; help others to stop procrastinating; help people through tough times; motivate chronically underperforming employees; motivate salespeople; manage your stress.

Time

5–10 minutes.

What You'll Need

No special materials are needed.

What to Do

Explain the basics of the "cleansing breath":

First we're going to inhale very deeply—in fact, we're going to take a huge noisy breath in, exaggerating the effort. I'll demonstrate shortly. Second, we're going to hold that breath to a slow count of five. And, finally—and this is the good part—we're going to exhale very, very slowly, and, as we do so, we're going to blow away all of the tension in our bodies, until we've exhaled fully.

Now demonstrate a cleansing breath, and then talk the group through two or three breaths. Ask people how the cleansing breath made them feel. Most people will report feeling very relaxed.

Finally, lead a discussion about how the cleansing breath might be used during the day to help combat de-motivators!

Discussion Questions

1.   Would you be reluctant to do a cleansing breath at work? Why or why not?
2.   What are situations in which the cleansing breath might be useful for you? What are situations where you would be reluctant to use the cleansing breath?
3.   What are advantages and disadvantages of the cleansing breath as a stress-management technique?

Personal Touch

The cleansing breath is also effective when you are at home. Let the deep, refreshing breath be part of your morning routine to prepare for the day ahead.

THE CAREFUL CRITIQUE GAME

In a Nutshell

Participants critique a Brave Volunteer's speech using special guidelines.

What It's For

Use this game if you want to: overcome anxiety and the fear of failure; motivate your staff members to perform at their peak; improve your managerial skills; help managers improve their managerial skills; motivate chronically underperforming employees; spark peak team performance; help a team set and meet goals; motivate people in a large organization, design a motivating environment.

Time

20–30 minutes.

What You'll Learn

Participants learn the difference between destructive and constructive criticisms.

What You'll Need

Copies of the handout on page 60 for all participants.

What to Do

Remind participants that when feedback cannot be positive, it should at least be constructive. Constructive criticism identifies and sometimes praises current performance levels and then suggests ways to improve.

Next, find a Brave Volunteer to give a 5-minute speech to the group on a topic of his or her choice. Divide the group into small teams, and distribute worksheets to each team which list examples of constructive and destructive criticism (see the handout on page 60). Explain that after the speech, the teams should list at least five destructive criticisms and at least five constructive criticisms of the speech. Now have the Brave Volunteer deliver the speech.

Give the teams about 10 minutes to make their lists, and then call on representatives from a few teams to report on their results. Lead a brief discussion about the advantages of constructive criticism.

Discussion Questions

1. What is the difference between constructive criticism and destructive criticism?
2. What are some ways you can turn a destructive comment into a more constructive one?

3. Why do you think most criticism is destructive?

4. How can constructive criticism motivate?

Alternative

If your participants are a little shy, give the presentation yourself! Then distribute the handouts and ask the participants to critique your speech.

If You Have More Time

Repeat the process with other Brave Volunteers.

TYPES OF CRITICISM

Destructive	Constructive
"Not enough eye contact."	"Good eye contact. Do more."
"Posture was awful."	"You can look more confident by standing straighter."
"You spoke too fast."	"Try slowing down a bit."
"Your speech was too short."	"I would've liked to hear more."
"You were so boring."	"It might be helpful to involve your audience more."
"You mumbled."	"Speak a little louder so the people in the back can hear you too."

THE COLOR OF MOTIVATION

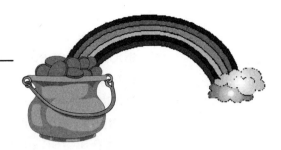

In a Nutshell

Participants sort color tiles in order from least motivating to most motivating.

What It's For

Use this game if you want to: perform at your peak; boost your energy when it's low; fight boredom; motivate your staff members to perform at their peak; spark peak team performance; help a team set and meet goals; motivate people in a large organization; jump-start your creativity; design a motivating environment.

Time

5–10 minutes.

What You'll Learn

Color can greatly affect mood—and energy!

What You'll Need

Each participant will need an envelope containing small (about 2 inches square) color tiles, which can easily be made with a paper cutter. Each set of tiles should be identical and should contain eight tiles: black, white, and six basic rainbow colors (violet, blue, green, red, orange, and yellow). They can be stored and later distributed in small envelopes.

What to Do

Remind participants that properly designed work spaces can create a sense of energy and improve productivity. Studies show that the colors that surround us—the colors of the walls, the colors of the furniture, and so on—have a significant impact on mood and performance. Both hue (color) and intensity (brightness) can make a difference. Generally, intense colors produce more energetic reactions, as do "hot" colors like reds and yellows. (There are exceptions to this rule, and different people react differently to different colors.) Using color wisely can help produce an atmosphere in which concentration, learning, and motivation can flourish.

Distribute the color packets, and ask people to sort the colors in order from what appear to be the *most energizing* to the *least energizing*. Get a show of hands to determine which color is considered the most energizing the most frequently. Also determine which color is considered the least energizing.

Finally, lead a discussion about how to design or modify a work environment so that color is used to increase energy, motivation, and performance.

Discussion Questions

1. Which colors tend to energize you when you need to be energized?
2. Are there certain colors, textures, or patterns that make you feel stressed? That make you feel relaxed?
3. How can we accommodate people whose color preferences don't fit the norm?
4. What are some advantages and disadvantages of decorating the workplace exclusively in energizing colors? Exclusively in soothing colors?
5. How might the colors in your workplace currently be affecting mood and performance? How can you improve the color scheme?

Alternative

Bring a lamp and some colored bulbs with you to the training room. Extinguish the room lights and illuminate the room in blue, red, or other colors. Ask people for their reactions to various colors.

If You Have More Time

Divide the group into teams of four or five people, and give the teams 15 minutes to plan ideal color schemes for their work environment. Have a representative of some or all of the teams report his or her team's recommendations to the entire group. You can also expand the game by increasing the number and variety of color tiles.

Personal Touch

Order your own set of color tiles. Then decorate your home and work spaces to achieve the energy—or the calm—that you desire.

CROSSING THAT BRIDGE

In a Nutshell

Teams compete with individuals in a bridge building contest.

What It's For

Use this game if you want to: motivate your staff members to perform at their peak; help managers improve their managerial skills; spark peak team performance; help a team set and meet goals; motivate people in a large organization; motivate salespeople; use competition as a motivational tool.

Time

15 minutes (or more, if you choose to do more rounds).

What You'll Learn

Some goals can be reached only when people work together.

What You'll Need

You'll need rulers, a whistle, and lots of colorful foam "bathtub blocks" (available in many toy stores or at websites such as poof-toys.com).

The blocks, all of which are about 1-inch thick, come in a variety of shapes. You'll need to create identical sets of blocks for each team. In each set, you might want to include the following blocks:

(2)	6-inch by 1.5-inch rectangles
(4)	3.5-inch by 1.5-inch rectangles
(4)	3-inch by 1.5-inch rectangles
(1)	3-inch square
(2)	triangles
(2)	half-circles
(2)	circles

What to Do

Divide the group up as follows: Some participants (say, 10 or so) will remain working on their own, outside of teams; in effect, each person will be a one-person team. Divide the remainder of the group into teams of between three and five people. Now distribute one set of blocks to each team, including to each of the one-person teams.

Inform the participants that their task is to use the blocks to build the *widest possible bridge* that they can. In several successive 3-minute rounds, have both types of teams (multi-member and one-member) build a bridge, and then measure the widths. Announce the winner, record the results on a blackboard or flipchart, and compute the average width for each type of team. Generally the multi-person teams will build much wider bridges than the individuals can build, mainly because on a team, one person can steady a structure while another person adds anchors of various sorts.

Repeat the procedure for as many rounds as time permits, and lead a discussion about why a team effort is essential in this and a wide variety of other tasks.

Discussion Questions

1. Did the teams perform differently from the individuals? How so?
2. What is the advantage of working in teams?
3. When is it more motivating to work in a team? When is it more motivating to work as an individual?

Alternative

If your game budget is slim, have one multi-person team compete against an individual, while the rest of the group looks on.

Tip!

This game is a variation on "Bridges to Creativity," a game that appears in Dr. Epstein's book, *The Big Book of Creativity*

Games. In that game, one team is given "open-ended" instructions—like the instructions used in this chapter—and a second team is given "bounded" instructions—the kind that imply a limit. Open-ended instructions ("Give me as many names as you can for this product" or "Build the widest possible bridge you can") usually produce more and better solutions than do bounded instructions ("Give me three new names for this product" or "Build a bridge that spans this river"). If you want to teach people about the importance of open-ended instructions, try "Goal-a-Rama IV" (page 101).

THE CRYSTAL BALL GAME

In a Nutshell

Participants gather around a crystal ball while they concentrate on positive futures.

What It's For

Use this game if you want to: perform at your peak; stop procrastinating; boost your energy when it's low; envision and achieve your personal goals; overcome anxiety and the fear of failure; motivate your staff members to perform at their peak; help managers improve their managerial skills; help others to stop procrastinating; help people through tough times; motivate chronically underperforming employees; help a team set and meet goals; motivate people in a large organization; motivate salespeople.

Time

20–30 minutes.

What You'll Learn

The motivating power of concentrating on a bright future.

What You'll Need

You'll need one crystal ball and one small table for every small team of three to five people. For extra fun, dress as a colorful fortune-teller during the game. Another fun option is to have one colorful scarf per table, to be worn by the designated "Madame Fortuna."

What to Do

Divide the group into teams of between three and five people, and have each team choose one member to be Madame Fortuna, the mysterious fortune-teller of bright futures.

Instruct the various Madame Fortunas to put one hand on the crystal ball, point to someone at the table—the "Chosen One"—and recite:

> "Into the Future I see...
> All that you will ever be—
> Smiles and riches are you,
> Success and happiness too!"

The Chosen One then puts his or her hand on the crystal ball. For the next minute or so, that person, along with everyone else in the group, stares at the crystal ball and tries to focus on a bright future for the Chosen One.

Madame Fortuna then asks the Chosen One what he or she saw, asks others to add more details, and then adds details of his or her own. The Chosen One then becomes Madame Fortuna for the next round of fortune telling.

Finally, ask for a brief report from a representative of each of the teams, and lead a discussion about the motivating power of visualizing a bright future.

Discussion Questions

1.   What bright futures did you see?
2.   How did it feel when other focused on your future?
3.   Why is it important to visualize a bright future?

If You're Short on Time

Pick a small group of people to demonstrate this on a stage for other participants to watch. To move things a little faster, play Madame Fortuna yourself.

DIFFERENT STROKES

In a Nutshell

Participants complete a special survey
that shows how dramatically one person's motivators differ
from another person's motivators.

What It's For

Use this game if you want to: improve your managerial skills;
help managers improve their managerial skills.

Time

20–30 minutes.

What You'll Learn

Motivators differ dramatically from one person to another.

What You'll Need

Copies of the survey form on page 77 for all participants,
along with writing materials.

What to Do

Divide the group into small teams of equal size—five people per team is ideal for this game. If you can, make each team as diverse as possible.

Next, distribute the survey form (see page 77) to all participants. On the top part of each form, every individual should simply list his or her favorite ice cream, sport, activity, food, and color.

Then one person on each team should compute the team's Agreement Scores. These scores reflect how many pairs of people have the same preferences. In a group of five people, one way to compute an Agreement Score for ice cream is to draw a pentagon and label each vertex with the appropriate flavor. If no one agrees, for example, the Agreement Score is 0:

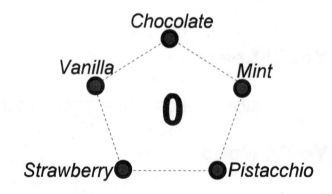

If two people agree on chocolate and three agree on mint, then the Agreement Score is 4:

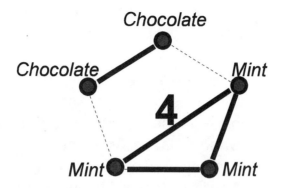

The scoring sheet on page 77 lists the scores that result from every possible combination of agreements that can occur on teams of between three and five people. You can compute the scores by referring to the chart on the scoring sheet, or, for fun, you can have people draw pentagons (for groups of five), rectangles (for groups of four), or triangles (for groups of three) and then connect the dots.

In a given category (say, ice cream) for a group of five people, the lowest possible Agreement Score is 0 and the highest is 10. The scorer should compute Agreement Scores for each of the five categories, as well as a Total Agreement Score for his or her team. The minimum possible Total Agreement Score for a team is 0, meaning no agreement. Because there are five categories, the maximum possible Total Agreement Score for teams of three, four, and five people, are 15, 30, and 50, respectively. The scores on each team will probably fall far short of the possible maximums. The lower the scores, the more diverse people's tastes.

After the scoring is complete, lead a discussion about the significance of the results.

Discussion Questions

1. What were the Agreement Scores for your team? What was your Total Agreement Score? How far was this from the maximum possible score?
2. What do these Agreement Scores tell you about the diversity of people's tastes?
3. Why is it important to understand what motivates other people?

Tip!

An individual's motivators change from time to time. It's important in organizations or at home to monitor people's changing tastes. Also, keep in mind that the scores you get in this game will be artificially high if your teams are homogeneous. If people self-select their teams (see "The Dream Team," page 79), their teams might end up being more homogeneous. The results in this game will tend to be more dramatic if you assign people to their teams.

MOTIVATOR SURVEY

1. Your favorite ice cream: _____
2. Your favorite sport: _____
3. Your favorite activity: _____
4. Your favorite food: _____
5. Your favorite color: _____

Agreement Scores

Directions: First, find your team size below. Then find the pattern that fits your results in each category (for example, if your team has five members, and they picked Mint-Mint-Mint-Chocolate-Chocolate, the pattern is AAABB). Write the corresponding Agreement Score in the space on the right. Finally, add up the Agreement Scores to get the Total Agreement Score for your team.

Group Size	*Pattern*	*Agreement Score*	*Team Scores*				
3	ABC	0					
	AAB	1					
	AAA	3	Ice Cream	Sport	Activity	Food	Color
4	ABCD	0					
	AABC	1					
	AABB	2	Ice Cream	Sport	Activity	Food	Color
	AAAB	3					
	AAAA	6					
5	ABCDE	0					
	AABCD	1					
	AABBC	2	Ice Cream	Sport	Activity	Food	Color
	AAABC	3					
	AAABB	4					
	AAAAB	6					
	AAAAA	10					

Total Agreement Score: _____

77

THE DREAM TEAM

In a Nutshell

Some people volunteer to serve on teams, while others are drafted, and then they rate their satisfaction.

What It's For

Use this game if you want to: improve your managerial skills; help mangers improve their managerial skills; spark peak team performance; help a team set and meet goals.

Time

10 minutes.

What You'll Learn

People are generally more enthusiastic about being on a team if they've been able to "self-select"—to choose their own teammates—rather than being assigned to a team.

What You'll Need

Copies of the questionnaire on page 81.

What to Do

First divide the group in half. The first half will be the Volunteers, and the second half will be the Draftees—but don't tell the groups until later!

Now pass out random numbers to assign the Draftees to teams of between four and six people. Next, let the Volunteers break up into teams of between four and six people.

Now ask all team members (in both groups) to complete a brief questionnaire (page 81). Then have a member of each team tabulate total scores for each question, mean scores for each question, a total mean score for the Draftees, and a total mean score for the Volunteers.

The Volunteers will probably outscore the Draftees on every question and overall, meaning that they're happier with their groups than the Draftees are. Lead a brief discussion about the results.

Discussion Questions

1. Which teams scored higher, the Volunteers or the Draftees? Why the difference?
2. Why do people prefer being on teams that they've chosen to join?
3. What are some advantages of self-selection? What are some disadvantages?

TEAM CHECKUP!

1. What is your comfort level with this team?
   Low 1   2   3   4   5   High

2. How enthusiastic are you about being on this team?
   Low 1   2   3   4   5   High

3. How much do you trust the other team members?
   Low 1   2   3   4   5   High

4. How high is your loyalty to this team?
   Low 1   2   3   4   5   High

5. How well do you think you'll be able to perform on this team?
   Low 1   2   3   4   5   High

6. How well do think your fellow team members will be able to perform?
   Low 1   2   3   4   5   High

7. How well do you think this team will be able to handle internal conflicts that might arise?
   Low 1   2   3   4   5   High

ERGONOMETRY

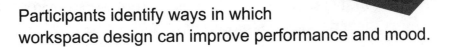

In a Nutshell

Participants identify ways in which workspace design can improve performance and mood.

What It's For

Use this game if you want to: perform at your peak; improve your managerial skills; help managers improve their managerial skills; motivate people in a large organization; manage your stress; design a motivating environment.

Time

15 minutes.

What You'll Learn

The right furniture or tools can make work easier to handle and keep you more productive.

What You'll Need

Participants will need writing materials.

What to Do

Remind participants that providing a comfortable workplace can boost morale and increase productivity.

Have people write down at least one comfort-inducing change that could be made in their current work environment. Ask a few people to share their ideas.

Here is a list of simple devices that can be added to an office environment to make life easier. Add other examples as you learn about them, especially if they're suggested by members of your group.

> *A headset attachment for the telephone*
> *A touch pad*
> *A trackball mouse*
> *An ergonomic keyboard*
> *A vibrating back massage device*
> *A glare-reduction screen*
> *A footrest, to ease lower back strain*
> *An under-the-desk keyboard drawer*
> *A chair pillow, to support the lower back*
> *Desk chairs with adjustable heights*
> *Shelving and containers that keep*
>   *frequently used objects close by*

Discussion Questions

1. How do your present working conditions affect your mood and performance?

2.   What changes can be made in your work environment to make you feel more comfortable?

3.   Which of your proposals are most feasible? Which are least feasible?

Tip!

Keep individual differences in mind; what's irritating to one person might be soothing to another.

Personal Touch

How can you make your training environment, your home, and your office more comfortable? Make your own list!

FEED ME!

In a Nutshell

People try to guess pre-selected alphabet letters based on positive feedback from a partner.

What It's For

Use this game if you want to: boost your energy when it's low; improve your managerial skills; help managers improve their managerial skills; help others to stop procrastinating; motivate chronically underperforming employees; spark team performance; motivate people in a large organization; use competition as a motivational tool.

Time

20 minutes.

What You'll Learn

Positive feedback boosts performance, and it also can be fun!

What You'll Need

You'll need one large bowl and a bag of candies or popcorn for every pair of individuals who will be participating in the game. One person in each pair should also have some writing materials (a pad and pencil will do).

What to Do

Divide the group into pairs. If possible, have each pair of individuals sit on the floor, cross-legged, facing each other, not more than three feet away from each other. One person, the Listener, holds the bag of popcorn or candy, and the other person, the Speaker, holds the bowl.

Ask the Listeners to write down an alphabet letter of their choice and then to conceal that letter. The Speaker's job is to guess that letter. He or she can get clues about the letter by saying any three-word phrase aloud.

The Speaker begins the exchange by saying a three-word phrase. If the Listener throws a candy and the Speaker catches it, the Speaker can then guess a letter. If the Speaker misses, no guess can be made. If no candy is thrown, the Speaker can try another phrase.

When the correct letter is guessed, the exchange ends, and the Listener raises his or her hand to signal the successful conclusion of the exchange. Bonus: The Speakers can keep any candy they can catch! If time permits, have the Speaker and Listener keep switching roles, and play again!

Discussion Questions

1. How long did it take you to guess the target letters?
2. What impact did the positive feedback have on your performance?
3. What impact did the positive feedback have on your thinking? How did it affect the Speaker's phrases?
4. Why is positive feedback important for performance?
5. How can you increase your use of positive feedback in the workplace or at home?

Alternative

To make the game tougher, forbid the Listeners from selecting vowels or require the Speakers to use four- or five-word phrases. To make the game easier, allow the speakers to use two-word phrases or even single words. For extra fun, have the Speaker and Listener sit farther apart. If you're using popcorn, have the Listener aim for the Speaker's mouth!

If You Have More Time

Have participants switch partners!

GOAL-A-RAMA I

In a Nutshell

People toss pennies into bowls, having first been given no goal, a vague goal, or a clear goal.

What It's For

Use this game if you want to: stop procrastinating; boost your energy when it's low; envision and achieve your personal goals; improve your managerial skills; help managers improve their managerial skills; help others to stop procrastinating; help people through tough times; motivate chronically underperforming employees; spark peak team performance; help a team set and meet goals; motivate people in a large organization; motivate salespeople; use competition as a motivational tool.

Time

10 minutes.

What You'll Learn

Clear goals boost performance. The absence of goals is deadly.

What You'll Need

You'll need masking tape; small boxes, containers, or bowls; and lots of small candies, popcorn, chips, or pennies.

What to Do

Make a long line on the floor with the masking tape, and place several bowls on one side of the line, spaced two or three feet apart from each other, about five feet from the line (adjust the distance to make the task somewhat challenging).

Have some participants stand in a row on the other side of the line, and give them candies, popcorn, or pennies to toss into the bowls.

Instruct them exactly as follows: "Here are some pennies. There are some bowls." Now see how many pennies they get into the bowls over the next minute. Record that number on a blackboard or flipchart for all to see.

If necessary, empty the bowls, and give people more pennies. Now instruct them as follows: "This time, see if you can throw some pennies into the bowls. Ready, begin." After 1 minute has passed, stop the throwing, and count the number of pennies in the bowls. Write that number on the blackboard.

Empty the bowls, and give people more pennies, This time, say: "You just threw a total of [say the number] pennies into the bowls. Your goal now is to throw *as many pennies as possible* into each bowl, and make sure you throw more pennies into the bowls than you did last time." After a minute, stop the throwing, and count the pennies in the bowls. The total should be dramatically larger than the previous one.

Lead a discussion about the important of goal setting, and especially about the advantage of using clear goals rather than vague ones.

Discussion Questions

1. Which instructions worked better? Why?
2. How is performance affected when no goals are stated? When goals are vague? When goals are clear?

Alternative

If space allows, have three separate groups do the task simultaneously, with each group in a different area of the room. Give each group its instructions in writing. (This procedure controls for the "practice" effect: A single group will tend to do better after each round, even if the instructions don't change.)

GOAL-A-RAMA II

In a Nutshell

Participants identify and review different types of group reward systems and find possible improvements for the systems in use in their work environments.

What It's For

Use this game if you want to: motivate your staff members to perform at their peak; improve your managerial skills; help mangers improve their managerial skills; motivate chronically underperforming employees; spark peak team performance; help a team set and meet goals; motivate people in a large organization; motivate salespeople; design a motivating environment.

Time

30 minutes.

What You'll Learn

Different types of group goals can boost performance in different ways.

What You'll Need

Writing materials, handouts, or an overhead based on the figure on page 98.

What to Do

Remind participants that payoffs for good performance in a group can be arranged in a number of different ways. Three types of reward systems are shown in the figure on page 98. You might want to distribute copies of this or use it as an overhead.

The first two systems are fairly common. "One-to-one" is typical of many commission systems, and "many-to-many" is common in team-driven sales environments. The "one-to-many" system is less common, but has some advantages over the other systems (see the figure).

After reviewing these reward systems, have people meet in small teams to (a) identify and review the systems that are currently used in their work environments, and (b) discuss possible improvements in these systems. Call on a representative from some or all of the groups to summarize the findings of those groups, and lead a brief discussion about how different reward systems can be used to boost team performance.

Discussion Questions

1. What type of group reward system is currently in use in your workplace?
2. Do different group reward systems work better for different people and work environments? How so?
3. How can you improve the group reward systems currently in use in your workplace?

GROUP REWARD SYSTEMS

System	Goal Criterion	Reward	Outcomes
One-to-One (e.g., commission system)	One person meets a specified goal.	Only that person is rewarded.	*People are reluctant to help each other.* *People compete for resources.* *Only some individuals perform at a high level.*
Many-to-Many (e.g., team commission)	Combined performance of the group meets a specified goal.	Everyone is rewarded.	*People help each other.* *People share resources.* *Some people slack off.*
One-to-Many (e.g., commission sharing)	One person meets a specified goal.	Everyone is rewarded.	*People help each other.* *People share resources.* *Each individual performs at a high level.*

GOAL-A-RAMA III

In a Nutshell

Participants review current goal-setting practices in their workplace and seek to apply practices of Management by Objectives.

What It's For

Use this game if you want to: overcome anxiety and the fear of failure; motivate your staff members to perform at their peak; improve your managerial skills; help mangers improve their managerial skills; motivate chronically underperforming employees; spark peak team performance; help a team set and meet goals; motivate people in a large organization; motivate salespeople; design a motivating environment.

Time

30 minutes.

What You'll Learn

"Joint goal setting" by employees and managers can increase motivation and boost performance.

What You'll Need

Writing materials for all participants.

What to Do

Remind participants about the motivating value of joint goal setting, also called Management by Objectives (MBO). First introduced by Peter Drucker in the 1950s, this process lets employees negotiate achievable goals.

Now divide the group into small teams, and have the teams review current goal-setting practices in their workplaces and suggest improvements that incorporate MBO. Then call on representatives from some or all of the groups to summarize the results, and lead a brief discussion about the advantages and disadvantages of joint goal setting.

Discussion Questions

1. What are some advantages of joint goal setting?
2. Is joint goal setting being used in your workplace? How is it applied? How might it be applied more effectively?

GOAL-A-RAMA IV

In a Nutshell

Working in teams, participants invent names for a new hamburger. Some teams are given "open-ended" instructions, while other teams are given traditional, bounded instructions.

What It's For

Use this game if you want to: motivate your staff members to perform at their peak; improve your managerial skills; help mangers improve their managerial skills; motivate chronically underperforming employees; spark peak team performance; help a team set and meet goals; motivate people in a large organization; motivate salespeople; jump-start your creativity; design a motivating environment.

Time

20 minutes.

What You'll Learn

Open-ended instructions—ones that use phrases like "at least" or "as many as possible"—boost both creativity and performance.

What You'll Need

Writing materials should be provided for all participants. Also, you'll need written instructions for all of your teams: one set for the Crazy Creators and another set for the Daffy Designers. You can copy and cut the instructions on page 105 for this purpose.

What to Do

Divide the group into two subgroups, the Crazy Creators and the Daffy Designers, and divide each subgroup into teams of between three and five people.

Describe the task as follows: Sam, headstrong head of Research and Development, has developed a new low-calorie hamburger, which, of course, he'd like to call "Sam's Ham." You need to convince him that he's on the wrong track.

Distribute appropriate written instructions (see page 105) to each of the Crazy Creator and the Daffy Designer teams, and have the teams follow those instructions to prepare for their meeting with Sam.

Give the teams 15 minutes to carry out their instructions. Then call on representatives from some or all of the teams to present their reports. Keep track of two key numbers as each team presents its report: (1) the total number of new hamburger names developed in each group, and (2) the number of "fantastic" hamburger names developed in each group. Determine which type of team, on the average, performed better—the Crazy Creators or the Daffy Designers?

Explain to everyone how the instructions differed in the two subgroups, and summarize the numbers you have collected. It's likely that the Crazy Creators—the teams receiving open-ended instructions—will have produced (1) more hamburger names (on the average) and (2) more "fantastic" hamburger names (on the average) than were produced by the Daffy Designers—the teams receiving traditional bounded instructions.

Lead a discussion about why open-ended instructions—instructions that explicitly say that solutions should be unlimited in one or more ways—produce more and better outcomes than do traditional bounded instructions—instructions that either state or imply boundaries on creativity and performance.

Discussion Questions

1. Did the groups perform differently? How so?
2. What are open-ended instructions? How are they different from traditional instructions?
3. What types of instructions, goals, and tasks, are you usually given in your work setting—open-ended or bounded? Give some examples.
4. Why do open-ended instructions typically produce more and better ideas than do bounded instructions?

5. How might instructions in your work setting be improved to produce more and better ideas?

Alternative

If you like, you can also appoint a panel to judge the "creativeness" of the hamburger names produced by the two subgroups.

Instructions for the Crazy Creators

Sam, Director of R&D, wants to name his new hamburger "Sam's Ham." Fifteen minutes from now, a representative from your team must present Sam with a succinct report that will convince him to proceed with a better name. In the next 15 minutes, your team needs to invent as many new hamburger names as possible and then to present the following brief report to Sam:

> *Hi, Sam. We're pleased to report that our team has developed _____ [mention number here] possible new names for the company's new hamburger, _____ [mention number here] of which we think are truly <u>fantastic</u>. Our <u>fantastic</u> new hamburger names are _____ [give the names]. Thanks for your consideration!*

--✂

Instructions for the Daffy Designers

Sam, Director of R&D, wants to name his new hamburger "Sam's Ham." Fifteen minutes from now, a representative from your team must present Sam with a succinct report that will convince him to proceed with a better name. In the next 15 minutes, your team needs to invent five new hamburger names and then to present the following brief report to Sam:

> *Hi, Sam. We're pleased to report that our team has developed _____ [mention number here] possible new names for the company's new hamburger, _____ [mention number here] of which we think are truly <u>fantastic</u>. Our <u>fantastic</u> new hamburger names are _____ [give the names]. Thanks for your consideration!*

105

THE GOODFELLAS GAME

In a Nutshell

Participants find new and interesting
ways to reward good work.

What It's For

Use this game if you want to: boost your energy when it's low;
motivate your staff members to perform at their peak; improve
your managerial skills; help managers to improve their
managerial skills; help people through tough times; motivate
chronically underperforming employees; motivate people in a
large organization; motivate salespeople; jump-start your
creativity; design a motivating environment.

Time

30–45 minutes.

What You'll Learn

Performance can be rewarded in numerous—and sometimes
surprising—ways.

107

What You'll Need

No specific materials are needed, but you can add an element of fun by providing participants with writing materials, paste, construction paper, gold stars, and such.

What to Do

Select three volunteers to give brief, upbeat speeches to the group on any topic. After the first speech, ask members of the group to reward the speaker somehow—with praise, an object, a diagram, a promise, or something else—the more creative the better. If you like, provide a variety of materials to help participants create interesting rewards.

Each person in the group has to provide a different reward for the speaker. No one may repeat a previous reward. Call on at least five people before moving on to the next speech.

After the next speech, again call on at least five people to reward the speaker. Continue the process as time permits. Finally, lead a brief discussion about the value of rewarding people in new and interesting ways.

Discussion Questions

1. What were some of the interesting and novel ways in which participants rewarded the speakers?
2. How is behavior in your workplace currently rewarded?
3. What are some novel ways in which behavior in your workplace might be rewarded?

If You're Short on Time

Have one volunteer give a brief speech, and then solicit reward ideas from the group.

Personal Touch

If you find yourself using and getting the same old rewards, make a list of new ones you can give or would like to receive!

GROUP VS. TEAM

In a Nutshell

Groups compete with Teams in a fun football game.

What It's For

Use this game if you want to: motivate your staff members to perform at their peak; improve your managerial skills; help managers improve their managerial skills; spark peak team performance; help a team set and meet goals; motivate people in a large organization; use competition as a motivational tool.

Time

30–45 minutes.

What You'll Learn

A Group—an unstructured assemblage of people—is generally far less effective than a Team—a structured, organized assemblage in which roles are clearly defined.

What You'll Need

You'll need balloons or Nerf footballs—enough sets for everyone to play.   You'll also need a whistle.

What to Do

First of all, work out some simple rules for playing a football- or soccer-like game using balloons or Nerf balls.   You can do this with your participants; the rules will vary according to the space and time available.

Now divide the group into small teams of between four and six people. Half the teams are called Gaggles, and the other half are called Flocks.   Gaggle 1 will compete against Flock 1, Gaggle 2 against Flock 2, and so on. Competing teams need to be of equal size, and for every Gaggle, you need a Flock.

Each of the Flocks should be given an opportunity to meet for about 15 minutes in order to strategize and assign roles for the upcoming competition. Gaggles should not be allowed to meet as individual groups during this period. You might have all of the Gaggles mingle together on one side of the room, or simply give them a break outside the room.

After the Flocks have met, allow the Gaggles to form, and immediately begin the competition with a blow of your whistle.

The game should proceed in short rounds of no more than 5 minutes each. At the end of each round, get a quick count of the scores. In early rounds, Flocks should have the advantage. When the competition is over, lead a discussion about why the Flocks prevailed.

Discussion Questions

1. How does a group differ from a team?
2. How were the Flocks closer (at least in the early rounds) to a true team than were the Gaggles? Did this help the Flocks prevail over the Gaggles?
3. How does a group become a team?

Tip!

To try to ensure that Gaggles and Flocks are fairly equally matched in ability, consider assigning participants to one group or the other by flipping a coin or using some other method of random assignment.

HIGHER AND HIGHER

In a Nutshell

Participants envision a series of increasingly ambitious goals.

What It's For

Use this game if you want to: boost your energy when it's low; envision and achieve your personal goals; overcome anxiety and the fear of failure; motivate your staff members to perform at their peak; motivate chronically underperforming employees; spark peak team performance; motivate people in a large organization; motivate salespeople.

Time

15–20 minutes.

What You'll Learn

However high your current goals, you can raise them still higher.

What You'll Need

Copies of the handout on page 117.

What to Do

Distribute copies of the handout, and have participants spend about 10 minutes completing the form, briefly listing a series of increasingly ambitious goals for both their personal and professional lives.

When they're done, ask a few volunteers to share some items from their plans. Then lead a brief discussion about the importance that goals have for motivation.

Discussion Questions

1. How might higher goals lead to more motivation?
2. What are some wild goals you listed on your plan?
3. Were you surprised at any point by what you wrote on this plan? How so?
4. If goals are unrealistically high, might this hurt motivation?

Tip!

Many people don't have clear life goals, professional or personal. If participants seem stuck, encourage them to fantasize—even to identify with friends or characters in films or books.

Goal Plan!

Goal Level	Professional	Personal
Where I Am Now		
Reasonable Goals		
Higher Goals		
Even Higher Goals		
Obscenely High Goals		

THE I-DO GAME

In a Nutshell

Participants find commitment strategies for specific performances needing improvement.

What It's For

Use this game if you want to: perform at your peak; stop procrastinating; boost your energy when it's low; envision and achieve your personal goals; motivate your staff members to perform at their peak; help others to stop procrastinating; help people through tough times; motivate chronically underperforming employees; spark peak team performance; motivate people in a large organization.

Time

20 minutes.

What You'll Learn

One way to boost your performance is to make a specific commitment to another person or other people.

What You'll Need

You'll need writing materials and copies of the form on page 122 for all participants.

What to Do

Remind participants about the power of commitment. A commitment one makes to one's self, such as a New Year's resolution, can be helpful, but the commitment one makes to another person or to other people is often more powerful. Such a commitment is especially effective if you give other people the authority to act in some way, depending on how well you meet your commitment.

Distribute the planning form on page 122, and ask participants to spend about 10 minutes completing it. Then ask volunteers to present their plans, and lead a brief discussion about the power of commitment for boosting performance.

Discussion Questions

1. How can commitments improve performance? Have you used commitments in this way? What were the outcomes?
2. Do you have trouble making commitments? What seems to be stopping you?

Tip!

Many people are reluctant to make commitments to other people. Commitments can feel constraining, in part because they give other people a degree of power over the one who makes the commitment. The kind of commitments we're recommending here, however, are generated by the individual to help him or her achieve personal goals. In that sense, they exemplify good self-management. For further information, you may wish to consult Dr. Epstein's book *Self-Help Without the Hype*.

Personal Touch

You might want to consider demonstrating the power of commitment by making a personal commitment to the group! Could you use such a commitment in order to improve your own performance as group leader?

PLANNING FORM

Performance Needing Improvement	Commitment Strategy
1.	1.
2.	2.
3.	3.
4.	4.
5.	5.

I HAVE A DREAM

In a Nutshell

Through partially guided imagery,
participants visualize a wonderful scene in their future.

What It's For

Use this game if you want to: perform at your peak; stop procrastinating; envision and achieve your personal goals; overcome anxiety and the fear of failure; motivate your staff members to perform at their peak; help others to stop procrastinating; help people through tough times; motivate chronically underperforming employees; spark peak team performance; help a team set and meet goals; motivate people in a large organization.

Time

20 minutes.

What You'll Learn

Imagining a bright future can help you set inspirational goals.

What You'll Need

Writing materials for all participants.

What to Do

Part One: Have people get into a relaxed position. Ask them to breathe easily and close their eyes while you recite the following text in a soothing voice:

Breathe easily and clear your minds. I'm going to take you on journey. Just focus, concentrate on my voice and the feeling of relaxation that's beginning to grow in your body.... Keep relaxing....

Around you now is darkness.... You're completely surrounded by darkness.... You feel warm and comfortable, relaxed and at ease. Focus on your breathing. Make it slow and easy. Focus on the comforting blackness around you. Off in the distance, you see a small, round object. Slowly, gradually, it moves closer to you, until finally it's about three feet from you, suspended in the blackness, in front of your face. The object is a clock, and both of its hands are on the 12. It's a plain clock, with plain black hands on a plain...white...face.

You begin to feel that time has completely stopped as you continue to focus on the face of the clock, and its two hands, pointing upward toward the 12. Now, slowly, the minute hand begins to move clockwise around the dial, very slowly at first, then somewhat faster, and then faster still. In just a few seconds, it's moved completely around the dial, so that the hour hand is now on the 1. The minute hand continues to move, faster and faster and faster, so the hour hand moves from number to number to number with increasing speed.... As the hands continue to whirl around the face of the clock, you feel yourself being pulled...tugged gently into the future.... Wisps of air rush against your skin as you move forward through time...until, finally, you begin to slow down.... The hands of the clock have finally come to a complete stop, and 10 years have passed.

You look to your left, and off in the distance you see someone in a lighted area. It's you, in an ideal work situation, exactly 10 years from now. Everything is perfect in this work setting. Everything is ideal for you. Merge your awareness into the future you, and feel the warm, positive feelings of your future self. Now look around you. Who's with you? What kind of work environment do you see? What kind of equipment or furniture is there? Try to concentrate on the sounds. What are people saying? Is there a window? Can you see outside? If so, what do you see? Focus on whatever details you can see or feel or hear, and let yourself experience the fulfillment and pure satisfaction of your future self....

Now you feel yourself being pulled again into the darkness, until, off in the distance, another scene begins to emerge. Up ahead, you see yourself in another lighted area. This time, you're in an ideal situation at home, exactly 10 years from now. Everything is perfect.... Everything is ideal.... You're body is filled with warm, positive feelings.... Look around in that lighted area. Who's with you? What kind of furniture do you see? Try to concentrate on the sounds. Let the image grow clearer. Focus on whatever details you can see or feel or hear, and let yourself experience the feelings of satisfaction and fulfillment of your future self.

Now the lighted area darkens as you are gently, very gently, pulled into complete darkness again.... When I tell you to open your eyes, you'll be back in the present, and you'll remember the images you saw of your perfect future, and you'll retain those wonderful feelings of fulfillment and satisfaction.... Now, gradually, very gradually, open your eyes, and return to the present.

Part Two: Ask participants to jot down some of the details they saw in their images. Ask them to write a brief plan, indicating how they can get from where they are now to the ideal images they saw in their fantasy.

Finally, lead a brief discussion about the importance of both imagination and planning for motivation.

Discussion Questions

1. What images did you see in the lighted areas?
2. How did you feel when you saw those images?

3. Did the feelings of fulfillment and satisfaction persist after you opened your eyes?
4. How might visualizing a bright future help you improve your life?

Tip!

You can create a more intense experience by dimming the room lights and closing the windows and doors.

Personal Touch

Have someone read the above passage to you so you can visualize your own bright future!

KEEPING THE FIRES BURNING

In a Nutshell

Participants learn how to fight job burnout by envisioning and planning small changes in their workplace or job definition.

What It's For

Use this game if you want to: perform at your peak; stop procrastinating; envision and achieve your personal goals; overcome anxiety and the fear of failure; fight boredom; motivate your staff members to perform at their peak; improve your managerial skills; help managers improve their managerial skills; help others to stop procrastinating; help people through tough times; motivate people in a large organization; manage your stress.

Time

20–30 minutes.

What You'll Learn

Small changes can greatly affect your outlook!

What You'll Need

You might want to make overheads of pages 133 and 134.

What to Do

Explain to the participants that burnout is one of the most serious problems we face in the organizational environment, and its main cause is stress. Then proceed to explain that one key to fighting this stress is the Small-Change Principle, which is, like all good principles, quite simple: *Small changes can produce BIG outcomes* (page 133).

Show the overhead on page 134 to illustrate the Small-Change Principle. Seen right-side up, it looks like a happy face, but upside-down, it looks like a sad face.

Now present the following case to the group.

> *Suzanne had been an administrative assistant for five years, but gradually she had grown to hate her job. She felt that she was consistently treated unfairly, blamed for things that weren't her fault, and put under more pressure than she could bear. A consultant discovered that Suzanne made an average of 10 trips to the photocopy room each day, where she often encountered long lines or broken machines. Her boss was not very sympathetic, even though she told him about copy problems many times. The entire image she had of her job seemed to revolve around problems related to the copy machines. Rather than lose her,*

her boss agreed to provide a small copier for Suzanne's workstation. She felt vindicated, and, more important, the pattern of her workday changed dramatically for the better.

In your discussion, point out how small, isolated factors lead to very broad, overly general impressions of the workplace experience.

Following the discussion, have participants create a list of small changes they would like to see in their workplace that might make a big difference in their workplace experience. Have people share some of their suggestions, and explore the feasibility of implementing them.

Discussion Questions

1. What is burnout?
2. What is the Small-Change Principle? What are some examples?
3. How could the Small-Change Principle be used to protect you from burnout?
4. What are other ways to protect yourself from burnout?

If You're Short on Time

To make this a 10-minute exercise, (a) shorten the introduction, (b) have people make a list of small changes, and (c) call on a few people to share portions of their list with the group.

Tip!

Remember:

For want of a nail, the shoe was lost.
For want of a shoe, the horse was lost.
For want of the horse, the rider was lost.
For want of the rider, the message was lost.
For want of the message, the battle was lost.
For want of the battle, the war was lost.

THE <u>SMALL CHANGE</u> PRINCIPLE

"Small changes can produce **BIG** outcomes."

KING OF THE HILL

In a Nutshell

Participants take an imaginary journey to a kingdom where they're in charge and admired.

What It's For

Use this game if you want to: perform at your peak; boost your energy when it's low; fight boredom; help people through tough times; motivate chronically underperforming employees; spark peak team performance; motivate people in a large organization; motivate salespeople; test people's motivational skills.

Time

10 minutes.

What You'll Learn

Powerful, positive images can leave powerful, positive residual feelings.

What You'll Need

No special materials are needed.

What to Do

Ask participants to get into a relaxed position with their eyes closed. Next, take your participants on a journey by reciting the following text:

Now that you're sitting comfortably, I want you to listen very carefully as I take you on a beautiful journey. Now just relax, breathe easily, and clear your mind. Concentrate on my words and my voice. Here we go....

You're feeling calm and comfortable. Listen to yourself breathing in and out, slowly and easily.... With your eyes still closed and your body relaxed, slowly become aware of the sensations that surround you. A beautiful scene is slowly emerging.... You see clouds—soft, white, billowy clouds everywhere. You're up in the sky, high above everything. You feel yourself flying through the air, gliding easily. Feel the cool rush of wind surround you as you fly forward through the air.

Now look downward toward the ground. Below you are beautiful, green, rolling hills. In the distance, you spot the outlines of a grand castle standing majestically against the green hills. You draw closer, and now you see that the castle is made of magnificent grey stones.

You draw closer still, and now you're hovering over a royal courtyard, surrounded by grand red banners. You have a sense of anticipation, a sense that something wonderful is about to happen. You approach the large castle tower at the end of the courtyard, and you see beautiful stained glass windows decorating the castle walls. One large window is open. You fly through the window into the tower, and below you is a grand hall. Again, you feel a great sense of anticipation and wonder, as you begin to look around the great hall.

The ceiling is a hundred feet high, and great banners of many colors decorate the walls. A dozen enormous chandeliers hang from the ceiling, each lit by hundreds of sparkling lights. Below you is a long dining table, with a hundred colorfully dressed people standing by their chairs on each side of the great table. They're celebrating a great day and a great person. Everyone is facing the head of table, raising goblets of wine toward the person seated there. The scene glitters with gold and crystal and bright costumes and great plates of food. You continue to hover in the air over this majestic scene, your sense of exhilaration continuing to grow.

Slowly, you begin to move closer to the head of the table, toward the regal person seated there. Two hundred glasses are raised high toward this person, and the two hundred guests begin to cheer their admiration and approval. As the cheers grow louder, you finally see that you are the seated person whom everyone has come to admire. You feel your heart pounding with pride and wonder. As the cheers become almost deafening, you merge into the body, so that you now see the table and your admirers from the head of the table. Two hundred people drink to you. You focus on the faces of the people as they cheer and applaud. Pride and exhilaration fill you completely....

Now.... slowly, very slowly—and retaining a sense of pride and satisfaction—gradually, very gradually, open your eyes.

Discussion Questions

1. How did this journey make you feel?
2. Could you call up this image in the future?
3. How might this image help to motivate you?

Alternative

Try reciting this text on to an audio tape beforehand. Then all you'll need to do is press Play!

Tip!

Take care to make certain the environment is quiet for this session. Disturbances can spoil a grand journey.

MAKE ME LAUGH

In a Nutshell

Participants work in teams to explore ways in which humor can be used to improve unpleasant situations.

What It's For

Use this game if you want to: boost your energy when it's low; overcome anxiety and the fear of failure; help managers improve their managerial skills; help people through tough times; manage your stress.

Time

20–30 minutes.

What You'll Learn

Laughter can greatly improve energy level.

What You'll Need

Writing materials for participants.

What to Do

Remind participants how humor can be used to reinterpret what's happening or to defuse a tense situation.

Now, divide the group into teams. Have each team (a) write a description of three stressful situations (for example, interpersonal conflict, some problem with a boss, the failure of a project, or a tight deadline), and (b) explore ways in which humor might be used to improve the situation.

Call on a representative from some or all of the groups to report to the entire group, and lead a discussion about the outcomes.

Discussion Questions

1.   Has humor ever gotten you out of a tight spot? What happened?
2.   How might humor help in a tough situation? How might it hurt?

Alternative

You might want to have each team pick a scenario to role play. You can then have some teams present their role plays to the entire group.

THE MIDAS TOUCH

In a Nutshell

Participants imagine that they have a magic touch that can help them do amazing things.

What It's For

Use this game if you want to: perform at your peak; overcome anxiety and the fear of failure; motivate your staff members to perform at their peak; help people through tough times; motivate chronically underperforming employees; spark peak team performance; motivate people in a large organization; motivate salespeople; manage your stress.

Time

5 minutes.

What You'll Learn

An image that makes you feel powerful and effective can leave positive residual feelings.

What You'll Need

No special materials are needed.

What to Do

Advise participants to sit in a relaxed position, close their eyes, and breathe easily. Then begin in a soothing voice:

Listen closely, very closely, to my voice.... Breathe slowly and easily. Let your body relax. Here we go....

Envision yourself sitting at your desk. All around the desk, everything is in disarray. Papers are scattered everywhere on the desk. Stacks are piled high to the ceiling. A garbage can is overflowing with discarded papers. There's a computer on the desk, and it's been stricken with the blue screen of death. Everywhere you look you see chaos, and you find this disturbing, unsettling.

Suddenly, you feel a small tingle in your stomach. A new feeling begins to emerge, as the tingle spreads through your torso. It's a sense of power, a sense that you can make changes, a sense that you can triumph over chaos. Gradually, the feeling spreads to your arms and your hands, then upward to your neck and your head, then downward to your legs and feet. The feeling is energizing and warm and pleasant. As this warm, pleasant tingling lingers, you notice a dim golden glow at the end of your fingertips, a golden aura of power and energy.

Focus on this aura. Savor its warmth. Feel the power in your touch. Now look back to the desk, and reach over to a large stack of papers, touching it with your left index finger. The instant you touch the stack, all of the papers fly into the air, file drawers burst open around the room, and all of the papers rocket into their appropriate files. Some go straight to the garbage pail near your desk, which gives you a sense of great satisfaction. Now the golden glow around your fingertips grows brighter. You reach over to the computer and touch the blue screen with the same left index finger, and watch as the crashed computer comes back to life.... The pleasant tingling warmth in your fingertips is growing more intense, empowering you further. Now, reach out to a blank piece of paper on your left. Gently touch the paper with your index finger and, instantly, the paper fills with words, expressing your greatest thoughts. Feel the golden warmth tingling inside you, and relax....

Hold those warm, golden, powerful feelings inside you, as you slowly, very slowly, open...your...eyes....

Discussion Questions

1. How did this exercise make you feel? Did it energize you?
2. Could you call up this image in the future?
3. Did you feel any actual tingling in your fingers?

Alternative

You might want to put this image text on audio tape. That way you can just play the tape instead of reciting the text.

Tip!

Try to keep the environment relatively quiet. Distracting noises can spoil the journey for some people, so take care to close the doors and windows before starting.

Personal Touch

If you've put this image on tape, take it home and try it yourself!

THE MONOLOGUE GAME

In a Nutshell

Participants pair up to engage in alternating monologues.

What It's For

Use this game if you want to: improve your managerial skills; help managers improve their managerial skills; motivate salespeople.

Time

15 minutes.

What You'll Learn

To keep someone motivated, you need to be responsive to what he or she says.

What You'll Need

A timer would be helpful.

What to Do

Part One: Divide the group into pairs, and have the people in each pair face each other. Ask the pairs to engage in alternating monologues: The partners take turns speaking, but each person is unresponsive to the content of the other person's language. Instead, each person continues his own monologue, focusing only on his or her own thoughts and language.

Part Two: Ask the pairs to engage in a 3-minute conversation in which each person tries to be highly responsive to what the other is saying. Finally, lead a brief discussion comparing the two modes: responsive vs. unresponsive.

Discussion Questions

1.   Which mode is more motivating—the responsive mode or the unresponsive mode?
2.   Have you ever been unresponsive when speaking with someone? What was the outcome?
3.   Has someone ever been unresponsive when you spoke to him or her? How did this make you feel, and what was the outcome of the exchange?
4.   What is responsivity in conversation?
5.   It's impossible to be responsive unless you first listen carefully to what the other person is saying. Why?

Alternative

If you're working with a large group, have one pair of people demonstrate this phenomenon on stage.

If You Have More Time

If you've got spare time, add a third activity between parts one and two: medium responsivity. In this variation, each person responds both to the other person's language and to his or her own thoughts and language. Lead a brief discussion about the outcome.

Tip!

See "The Tiny Little Nod Game" on page 193 for more ideas!

THE MOVER-SHAKER GAME

In a Nutshell

Participants rate their energy level before and after vigorous exercise.

What It's For

Use this game if you want to: perform at your peak; stop procrastinating; boost your energy when it's low; feel less overwhelmed; overcome anxiety and the fear of failure; fight boredom; motivate your staff members to perform at their peak; help others to stop procrastinating; motivate chronically underperforming employees; motivate people in a large organization; motivate salespeople; manage your stress.

Time

15 minutes.

What You'll Learn

Short exercise breaks can greatly boost your energy level.

What You'll Need

You'll need copies of the energy scales for all participants (see page 152), a boom box, and some energizing tapes or CDs. ("She Works Hard for Her Money" is a good one!)

What to Do

Distribute copies of the energy scales to all participants. Then ask participants to rate their current energy level on a scale of 1 to 10, where 10 is the highest level of energy.

Next, turn on some fun music on your boom box and have people walk or run in place (depending on their ability) for about 3 minutes. Encourage participants to cheer each other on as they continue.

Now have them wait 30 seconds or so, and then ask them to rate their energy level once again. Compute a quick average, and, if you'd like, display the result on an overhead display. Has the average energy level increased?

Finally, explain the benefits of getting some brief exercise breaks during the work day. Vigorous physical activity can serve as a motivating force by improving overall health and well-being.

Discussion Questions

1. What effect does vigorous exercise have on your energy level?

2. Do you currently get any vigorous exercise during the work day, either at work or elsewhere? What kind and how much?

3. How might you incorporate vigorous exercise into your work day?

If You Have More Time

Here is a list of simple, non-taxing exercises that can be performed in an office environment. Add other examples as you learn about them, especially if they're suggested by members of your group.

Exercises

Knee lifts	*Stepping*
Jogging in place	*Bicycling*
Jumping jacks	*Rowing*
Twirling a hula hoop	*Dancing*

Personal Touch

Learn and practice your own movement routines to help you get motivated at home!

ENERGY SCALES

Rate your energy level before
and after some exercise:

0 ... *Comatose*
2 ... *Barely Breathing*
4 ... *So-So*
6 ... *Perky*
8 ... *Up & At 'Em*
10 ... *King of the World!*

Scale 1

```
|-----|-----|-----|-----|-----|-----|-----|-----|-----|
0     2     4     6     8     10
```

Scale 2

```
|-----|-----|-----|-----|-----|-----|-----|-----|-----|
0     2     4     6     8     10
```

THE NO-HANDS GAME

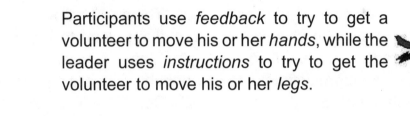

In a Nutshell

Participants use *feedback* to try to get a volunteer to move his or her *hands*, while the leader uses *instructions* to try to get the volunteer to move his or her *legs*.

What It's For

Use this game if you want to: improve your managerial skills; help managers improve their managerial skills; motivate sales people; use competition as a motivational tool.

Time

15 minutes.

What You'll Learn

Feedback is often a much more powerful motivator than rules or instructions—even instructions from an authority figure.

What You'll Need

Some *chutzpah* would be helpful.

What to Do

Pick a volunteer, then ask him or her to leave the room. Have the group pick a Target Behavior that uses *hands*, such as clapping overhead. Bring the volunteer back, and explain that the group is going to try to get him or her to do something that involves his *legs*. The group will shout "Yes!" whenever he or she does something close to the desired target. (This is called a "shaping" task, in which closer and closer approximations to a target behavior are reinforced, in this case with the word "Yes!" See "The Yes! Game" on page 217 for details.)

Because of the leader's instructions, the volunteer will keep moving his or her legs, but the group will shout "Yes!" only when he or she moves his or her *hands*. The feedback from the group will usually overwhelm the leader's instructions. The leader can interrupt at various points, insisting in increasingly stronger language that the group really wants the volunteer to move his or her *legs* and that he or she *mustn't* move his or her hands.

This game produces lots of tension and laughter, as the leader's instructions compete with the audience's feedback —with the feedback usually winning.

Discussion Questions

1. What happens when feedback competes with instructions? Which one usually wins?

2. What are examples from everyday life in which feedback is in competition with instructions?
3. What was the outcome of the game? What did it show about the power of feedback?
4. Why is it not enough for supervisors to ask people to get motivated? What else must they do to encourage motivation? How can feedback be used for this purpose?

Alternative

There are many possible variations. For example, the Target Behavior could involve legs rather than hands. As long as two incompatible behaviors are selected, the game should work well.

Tip!

Among other things, this game demonstrates why a manager's instructions are often ignored. Very often the natural consequences of behavior—the feedback people get—maintains behavior that's nothing like what the manager wants. This game also demonstrates why so many people ignore the warnings on cigarette packs.

POPEYE PUFFS

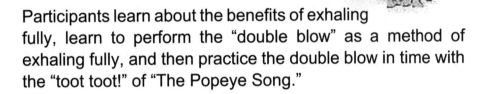

In a Nutshell

Participants learn about the benefits of exhaling fully, learn to perform the "double blow" as a method of exhaling fully, and then practice the double blow in time with the "toot toot!" of "The Popeye Song."

What It's For

Use this game if you want to: overcome anxiety and the fear of failure; feel less overwhelmed; improve your managerial skills; help people through the tough times; manage your stress.

Time

5–10 minutes.

What You'll Need

No special materials are required.

What to Do

First, explain the rationale: When the going gets tough, we tend to breathe shallowly, which means that we rebreathe excessively. Deliberately controlling one's breathing is a powerful way to keep control of one's mood, and the simplest way to assure the right mix of gases in your blood is to make sure that you occasionally *exhale fully*.

Next, explain and demonstrate the "double blow." When you forcibly blow out all of the air in your lungs, there's still some air left. In the double blow, we blow out all the air, and then, before we inhale, we blow hard once more. The torso is somewhat curled at this point, with the air apparently being expelled from the abdominal area. The point is to reset the respiratory system so that you stop rebreathing old air. Have people try this.

Finally—and have some fun with this—have the group sing "The Popeye Song," doing the double blow when Popeye normally does his "toot toot." Sing it a few times, with clapping, hand gestures, and body movement. Here is the basic verse:

> *I'm Popeye the sailor man, (puff puff)*
> *I'm Popeye the sailor man, (puff puff)*
> *I'm strong to the finish,*
> *'cause I eats me spinach,*
> *I'm Popeye the sailor man! (puff puff)*

Discussion Questions

1. What are the dangers of rebreathing? Of shallow breathing? Of hyperventilating?
2. Why is a double blow better than a single blow?
3. In what situations are you more likely to breathe improperly? How could you use the double blow as a quick corrective?
4. How long does it take to do a double blow? When might you use it during the day?

THE SLUMP GAME

In a Nutshell

Participants develop plans for keeping their motivation high when they're feeling low.

What It's For

Use this game if you want to: boost your energy when it's low; help people through tough times; motivate salespeople; manage your stress.

Time

15–20 minutes.

What You'll Learn

Planning ahead can help get you through the slow times.

What You'll Need

You'll need some version of the handout on page 164 for each participant.

What to Do

Distribute the form on page 164 (or some variation of it). Ask people to make a Slump Plan—a plan for coping with and overcoming a difficult period. Key areas to consider:

1) Resource identification and management
2) Stress management
3) Thought restructuring
4) Planning and goal setting

You might want to modify or expand the list based on the eight motivation competencies discussed in "Motivation Basics" (page 3) and "What D'Ya Know? (Individual Version)" (page 201).

After people complete the form, ask for some volunteers to share portions of their plans, and lead a discussion about slumps and how to beat them.

Discussion Questions

1. Have you ever been in a slump? What was the cause? How did you cope? What brought you out of the slump?
2. Might it be possible for you to fall into a slump in the future? What might put you there?
3. How might planning for the tough times help you? How might such planning help you even if tough times never occur?

If You're Short on Time

Make the handout on page 164 into an overhead, and briefly discuss it with participants.

Tip!

Planning for bad times can help you avoid them. Just as people believe that carrying an umbrella prevents rain, a plan for bad times can make people feel more confident and secure, which, in turn, can help them function more effectively.

Personal Touch

Your discussion might go better if you take a few minutes to complete your own Slump Plan before conducting the exercise. Feeling more secure?

SLUMP PLAN

Directions: *In each of the spaces below, indicate how you might be able to cope with and bounce back from a setback in your career or personal life.*

1. Resources

Whom can you count on to help? What material resources might you be able to fall back on?

2. Stress management

What techniques do you know that might help you get through a rough day? How might you be able to learn more techniques? What special activities might you engage in to make yourself feel better?

3. Thought restructuring

How might you able to reinterpret your difficulties in positive ways? For example, if your company goes bust, how might this be a good thing for you?

4. Planning and goal setting

How might planning and goal setting help you overcome your setback? Envision a crisis, and devise a brief plan that will help you prevail.

STACKED TO THE CEILING

In a Nutshell

Working together, participants help each other solve problems of disorganization.

What It's For

Use this game if you want to: overcome anxiety and the fear of failure; feel less overwhelmed; improve your managerial skills; help managers improve their managerial skills; help people through tough times; manage your stress.

Time

20 minutes.

What You'll Need

Copies of the handout on page 167 for every participant.

What to Do

Remind participants that *disorganization* is one of the major sources of stress in our lives. Anything you can do—even something very small—to get yourself better organized will likely reduce the stress you're feeling.

Distribute the handout on page 167 to the participants. Have a volunteer describe a problem of disorganization, and ask the group for fixes.

List these items on a display board, and from these suggestions create a second list that contains some general organizing principles. As time permits, repeat this process with other volunteers.

Discussion Questions

1. How can disorganization lead to stress?
2. What's your favorite trick or tool for getting organized?
3. What's your worst organizing problem? How might you solve it?

Tip!

Remember, *"People who keep lists of things to do, do more things."*

Personal Touch

Disorganized? Take yourself through the exercise by listing areas where you need improvement and seek ways to change.

GET ORGANIZED!

- CALENDERS, SCHEDULING SOFTWARE, PDAs
- LISTS OF THINGS TO DO
- LABEL TASKS WITH PRIORITY STATUS

- SEEK REMINDERS FROM COLLEAGUES
- POST NOTES, AFFIRMATIONS
- SEND YOURSELF NOTES, AFFIRMATIONS

- LEAVE MESSAGES ON YOUR VOICE MAIL
- CREATE ADEQUATE SHELF AND FILE SPACE
- KEEP FREQUENTLY USED ITEMS CLOSE BY

- KEEP IMPORTANT ITEMS IN SPECIAL PLACES
- SCHEDULE DAILY TIME FOR PLANNING
- ALWAYS CARRY A RECORDING DEVICE

- ALWAYS CARRY BACKUP BATTERIES
- MAKE DAILY, WEEKLY, MONTHLY, YEARLY PLANS
- DIVIDE UP DIFFICULT TASKS INTO SMALL ONES

- SCHEDULE EXERCISE TIME
- SCHEDULE RELAXATION TIME
- WHAT WORKS FOR YOU?

THE STAR CHART GAME

In a Nutshell

Participants find ways to self-monitor lagging performances.

What It's For

Use this game if you want to: perform at your peak; stop procrastinating; envision and achieve your personal goals; overcome anxiety and the fear of failure; motivate your staff members to perform at their peak; help others to stop procrastinating; help people through tough times; motivate chronically underperforming employees; spark peak team performance; motivate people in a large organization; motivate salespeople.

Time

15 minutes.

What You'll Learn

If you monitor your behavior, your performance is likely to improve.

What You'll Need

Copies of the planning form on page 171, as well as the overhead on page 172.

What to Do

Explain to participants that self-monitoring generally improves performance. Studies show that when people keep track of their progress, they usually progress more rapidly, and people can self-monitor using a wide variety of devices or personalized "star charts" (see page 172 for examples).

Distribute copies of the planning form on page 171, and have participants spend about 10 minutes completing it. Assure participants that you won't be collecting the forms.

Once they've finished, call on a few volunteers to share some items from their plans. Lead a brief discussion about the importance of self-monitoring for improving performance.

Discussion Questions

1.   Do you currently use self-monitoring to help you perform, or have you ever used this technique? How so, and how well does this technique work for you?
2.   How might you use self-monitoring to help you in the future?
3.   Were you surprised by anything you wrote on your planning form? Please explain.

PLANNING FORM

Performance To Be Improved	Self-Monitoring Method(s)
1.	1.
2.	2.
3.	3.
4.	4.
5.	5.

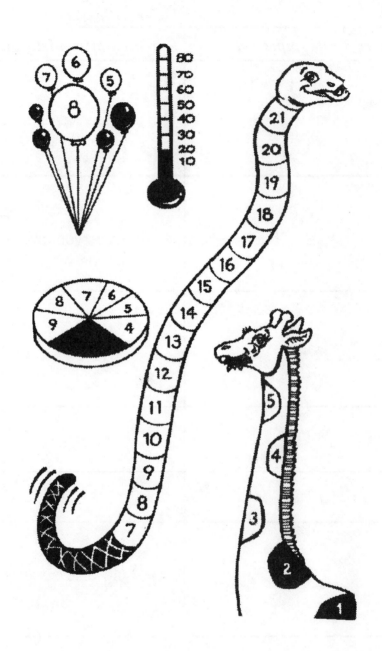

THE SUPERSTITION GAME

In a Nutshell

"Accidental reinforcers" are used to get a volunteer to behave in some wild and wacky ways in this upbeat game.

What It's For

Use this game if you want to: improve your managerial skills; help managers improve their managerial skills.

Time

15–20 minutes.

What You'll Learn

Even accidental consequences can have a tremendous impact on behavior.

What You'll Need

You'll need a table (or something else someone can hide behind) and some masking tape.

What to Do

Ask for a volunteer to serve as the Plucky Pigeon. Then send him or her out of the room. Next, tilt a table onto its side, and position it in the front corner of the room. With the masking tape, mark out a large rectangle (roughly 4 feet by 8 feet) on the floor in the front of the room.

Now ask for another volunteer to serve as the Fickle Feeder. He or she should then hide behind the table, positioned so that when the Plucky Pigeon enters the room, standing at any point in the rectangle, he or she will not be able to see the Fickle Feeder. Also, the Fickle Feeder should not be able to see the Plucky Pigeon.

Give the Fickle Feeder a pen, and indicate that every 5 or 10 seconds, he or she should raise the pen slightly over the edge of the table. Tell the group that whenever they see the pen go up, they should shout "Yes!" Practice this a few times with the group. Then tell the Fickle Feeder to refrain from raising the pen until after the Plucky Pigeon has returned to the room, you've given him or her some instructions, and you've said "Lets begin."

Now ask people in the audience to throw assorted objects (lipsticks, keys, watches, coins, etc.) into the rectangle.

Finally, escort the Plucky Pigeon into the room, position him or her in the rectangle and explain: "The group is going to try to get you to do something. When they see you doing anything close to the desired behavior, they'll shout 'Yes!' to let you know you're proceeding in the right direction. Your job is to try to discover the right thing to do just as quickly as you can, and you'll need to stay within this rectangle at all times. Any questions? Now, let's begin."

For the next few minutes, you'll probably see the Plucky Pigeon exhibit a variety of strange, funny, "superstitious behaviors." Every now and then, when he or she reaches for an object or bends in a certain way, the hidden Fickle Feeder will raise the pen, the group will shout *Yes!*, and the *Yes!* will accidentally reinforce whatever the Plucky Pigeon happened to be doing at that moment. You'll probably find the Plucky Pigeon repeating certain actions over and over—even though all of the reinforcers were actually coming at random times.

The group will probably have great fun with this. After 10 minutes or so, stop the game, and lead a brief discussion about the power of reinforcers—even accidental ones!

Discussion Questions

1. Did the reinforcers have an impact on the Plucky Pigeon's behavior, even though they were occurring accidentally? What kind of impact?
2. Could the Plucky Pigeon's behaviors be considered "superstitious"? How so?
3. Do you engage in behaviors of this sort in real life?
4. How do accidental consequences affect our everyday behavior—for example, in sports or recreational activities, in business, and at home?
5. How can we protect ourselves from accidental consequences?

Tip!

The key to success in this game is to make sure that the Plucky Pigeon and the Fickle Feeder are positioned so they can't see each other. Also, make sure that the Fickle Feeder raises his pen only slightly, so that the audience can see the movement but so that the Plucky Pigeon doesn't notice it. This probably sounds harder than it actually is. Try it! It's easy and fun!

TARGET PRACTICE

In a Nutshell

Participants learn how to identify and eliminate de-motivators in their professional and personal lives.

What It's For

Use this game if you want to: perform at your peak; feel less overwhelmed; overcome anxiety and the fear of failure; motivate your staff members to perform at their peak; improve your managerial skills; help managers improve their managerial skills; help people through tough times; motivate chronically underperforming employees; manage your stress; design a motivating environment.

Time

20 minutes.

What You'll Learn

Understanding what de-motivates you is essential to understanding what motivates you.

What You'll Need

Copies of the form on page 180 for all participants.

What to Do

Explain that we are often surrounded by de-motivators that hinder progress—and motivation. De-motivators are people, places, and things that irritate you, sapping your energy. For some people, working conditions might be "de-motivating"; for others, the problem might be peers. One way to increase motivation, then, is to identify and eliminate de-motivators.

Ask participants for examples of de-motivators. Then have them list some of their de-motivators in the left-hand column on the form (page 180), as well as constructive ways of eliminating or curtailing those de-motivators in the right hand column. Give people about 10 minutes to make their lists. Then call on volunteers to present some items from their lists, and ask for group reactions and comments.

Discussion Questions

1. Can all de-motivators in your environment be eliminated or curtailed? Which ones can? Which ones can't?
2. How can you curtail or eliminate de-motivators at work? At home?
3. Why is it important to identify de-motivators?

Alternative

You can jazz up this game by putting a real target on the wall, labeling different areas with the names of different de-motivators, and then having people throw Velcro or other projectiles at the target.

Personal Touch

Make a list of your own de-motivators, and try to devise ways of minimizing or eliminating them.   Share the outcome with your group.

Target Plan

De-Motivators	Plan of Attack!
1.	1.
2.	2.
3.	3.
4.	4.
5.	5.

THE TCHOTCHKE
GAME

In a Nutshell

Participants design Small-Reward Programs for their workplace.

What It's For

Use this game if you want to: motivate your staff members to perform at their peak; improve your managerial skills; help managers improve their managerial skills; motivate chronically underperforming employees; spark peak team performance; motivate people in a large organization; motivate salespeople; design a motivating environment.

Time

20 minutes.

What You'll Learn

Small rewards can produce big outcomes.

What You'll Need

You'll need a variety of attractive giveaway "tchotchkes" ("choch-kees"—Yiddish for knickknacks). Ideally, you'll need at least one for every participant. You'll also need writing materials for all participants.

What to Do

Begin by distributing the tchotchkes to the participants. Now, ask for specific reactions, such as: "How do the tchotchkes make you feel about me? How do they make you feel about the upcoming game?"

Lead a brief discussion about the possible value of small rewards, both tangible and intangible, both in the workplace and at home.

Now, break the group up into small teams and ask them to design Small-Reward Programs for their workplaces. Here are some examples of simple, small rewards:

> *Cookies with your logo baked in*
> *Key chains*
> *Mouse pads*
> *Water bottles*
> *Restaurant coupons*
> *Fresh flower, single stem*
> *Customized screen savers*
> *Baseball caps with logo*

Finally, call on representatives from some or all of the teams to report on their results.

Discussion Questions

1. What are the costs of a Small-Reward Program? What are the benefits?
2. Why are Small-Reward Programs in the workplace important for motivation?
3. How could you use small rewards in your workplace to improve morale and productivity?

Tip!

Try to get creative with your tchotchkes! Coffee mugs, pens, and notepads are safe standbys, but don't be afraid to try to find something unique!

THE TEN-YEAR PLAN

In a Nutshell

Participants complete a 10-year
personal and professional plan in order to
help them make decisions and keep perspective
on daily affairs.

What It's For

Use this game if you want to: perform at your peak; envision
and achieve your personal goals; motivate your staff
members to perform at their peak; help people through tough
times; motivate chronically underperforming employees;
manage your stress.

Time

20 minutes.

What You'll Need

Copies of the handout on page 188.

What to Do

Distribute copies of the handout, and give participants 10 to 15 minutes to complete it, briefly listing specific plans for both their professional and personal lives for the next 10 years. Assure participants that they'll be able to keep the forms; you won't be collecting them.

When they're done, ask a few volunteers to share some items from their plans. Ask people to share any surprises they may have experienced when completing the form. Ask for suggestions about how the plans might be used to help with daily planning. Consider various ways in which a long-term plan might be helpful; for example:

1. Attach it to a personal calendar to help stay on track.
2. Use it to help make daily decisions.
3. Use it to help keep minor problems in perspective.

Discussion Questions

1. How far ahead do you normally plan your life? Do you do this in writing?
2. What are some entries on your Ten-Year Plan? How clear were these ideas before you wrote them down? Did writing them down help to crystalize them?
3. Were you surprised at any point by what you wrote? How so?
4. How might you use a Ten-Year Plan to help you boost motivation or reduce stress?

Alternative

Depending on the group and the context, you might want to adjust the time period on the planner. Five years might be enough to prove your point. If your participants are very young, you might want to use a twenty-year planner.

Personal Touch

Don't forget to make your own Ten-Year Plan. It's a great way to get perspective on daily affairs.

TEN-YEAR PLAN

Starting Date:_____

Year	Personal Plan	Professional Plan
1		
2		
3		
4		
5		
6		
7		
8		
9		
10		

THINKING CAPS

In a Nutshell

Volunteers give speeches from wildly different perspectives in order to simulate a Job Exchange.

What It's For

Use this game if you want to: motivate your staff members to perform at their peak; help managers improve their managerial skills; motivate people in a large organization.

Time

20 minutes.

What You'll Learn

Role playing can be energizing, and a Job Exchange might help energize people at work.

What You'll Need

You'll need lots of hats! They can be homemade party hats (with labels on them that describe jobs or roles) or more elaborate costume-style hats (the kind used for Halloween).

Better still, get a variety of real hats from a secondhand store or hat store. Hats should suggest a wide range of different roles or jobs: adventurer, coach, detective, movie director, baseball player, cowboy, police officer, chef, etc. Wigs can also be employed. If all else fails, search your closets or attic. A large bucket, basket, or pail (large enough to hold all the hats) would be helpful. You'll also need at least a half dozen speech topic cards (see page 192 for ideas), which you should place in another container.

What to Do

Remind participants that people are often motivated by learning new things and by having opportunities to do new things. Now have volunteers come, one at a time, to the front of the room. Ask each volunteer to select a hat from the bin (raised up high so the hats can't be seen), and then ask him or her to draw a card from a second container (or hat!).

The volunteer's task is to give a 3-minute speech on the card topic from the perspective of a person who usually wears the hat.

Repeat the performance with other volunteers, hats, and cards, as long as time permits. Finally, lead a discussion about the possible value and potential feasibility of a Job Exchange program—a program in which people in different areas of an organization occasionally switch jobs for a day.

Discussion Questions

1. How easy was it for people to assume new roles and take on new tasks?
2. What are some advantages of letting people try new roles and tasks?
3. Is challenge always motivating? When is it not?
4. How feasible is it to employ a Job Exchange Program in your workplace?

Alternative

Attach job labels on hats, or simply have people pick Job Cards instead of selecting hats.

SPEECH TOPIC CARDS

Directions for Group Leader: Cut out some Speech Topics below and place them in a hat (or container.) After a volunteer has chosen a hat, have that person draw a Speech Topic card. If these topics don't work for you, make your own cards!

Improving Transportation Systems	Making Airline Travel More Comfortable
Designing a Better Bathroom	Reducing Pollution
The Ups and Downs of Time Travel	Improving the Postal Service

THE TINY LITTLE NOD GAME

In a Nutshell

People work in pairs, with one
person speaking and the other listening. The Listener tries
to get the Speaker to say a particular sentence, just by
nodding slightly from time to time.

What It's For

Use this game if you want to: improve your managerial skills;
motivate salespeople.

Time

15 minutes.

What You'll Learn

This verbal shaping game shows the power that even subtle
feedback has in encouraging creative speaking and thinking.
It also shows the power of positive reinforcement.

What You'll Need

Just a timer and some patience. A wristwatch will do—for the timer, not the patience.

What to Do

Divide the group into pairs. In each pair, one person is the Speaker and the other is the Listener. Have each Listener write down a Target Sentence—a non-obvious sentence that he or she would like the Speaker to say, such as "Ford makes a great car" or "I love pizza with mushrooms."

Then explain the task: Feedback—even subtle feedback—is so powerful that it can have an enormous impact on speech and thinking. The Speaker's task is to speak about anything and everyone for several minutes, watching for feedback from the Listener. The Listener's task is to "shape" the speech of the Speaker by reacting positively—with a *tiny little nod*—whenever the Speaker says something approaching the Target Sentence. No other feedback is allowed. Be sure to demonstrate the *tiny little nod* to the group.

When the Listener feels that the Speaker has reached or come very close to the Target Sentence (e.g., "My favorite car is a Ford"), the Listener should raise his or her hand to signal that his or her pair has completed the task. As each pair finishes, you can announce this to the group. Give the group 5 minutes to try to reach their Target Sentences. Add another minute or two if it looks some pairs are close to finishing.

Typically more than half of the pairs will reach the target within the allotted time—with most people amazed that subtle feedback can have such a large effect so very quickly.

Call on various pairs to reveal their Target Sentences and to report how close the Speaker came to reaching the target.

Discussion Questions

1. When you heard the instructions for this game, did you think it would work? Could a tiny little nod be sufficient to get someone to say an arbitrary sentence in a few minutes time?
2. How many pairs reached the Target Sentence? How many came close?
3. How do people provide subtle feedback in everyday life? How might this feedback be affecting people's speech and thinking?

Alternative

If you have more time, have the pairs switch Speaker and Listener roles.

Tip!

This is a remarkable game—short and simple, but with a big message about the enormous power of subtle feedback.

THE TWENTY-EIGHT-HOUR DAY

In a Nutshell

After reviewing some principles of time management, participants complete Time-Management Plans (TMPs), with the goal of adding 4 new hours to the day.

What It's For

Use this game if you want to: perform at your peak; stop procrastinating; feel less overwhelmed; motivate your staff members to perform at their peak; improve your managerial skills; help managers improve their managerial skills; help others to stop procrastinating; motivate salespeople; manage your stress.

Time

30 minutes.

What You'll Need

Writing materials for all participants, and copies of the handouts on pages 199 and 200.

What to Do

Review some major principles of time management. These techniques are summarized on page 199, which you might want to display.

Now have participants spend 15 minutes writing out a Personal Time-Management Plan (page 200). Have people list some time-management methods, along with the time they might save in a day by utilizing each of those methods. The goal is to add *four hours* to the day—about half of the traditional work day. Ask people for their totals. Ask where they had the most savings, whether the plan is feasible, and so on. You might want to compute a grand total on a blackboard or screen.

Discussion Questions

1. How would better time management help improve your day?
2. What are the impediments to better time management in your life? How can you defeat them?
3. How much time might you save with better time management? How might you spend that extra time?

Personal Touch

No group? Not to worry. Create your own TMP and devise ways to find those extra minutes.

Managing Time

- DELEGATE
- USE TECHNOLOGY WISELY
- USE COMMUTING TIME WISELY
- REDUCE MEETING TIME

- REDUCE INTERRUPTIONS
- REDUCE DISTRACTIONS
- CONTROL PAPERWORK
- SCHEDULE WISELY
- SCHEDULE LEISURE TIME

- SCHEDULE SCHEDULING TIME
- SCHEDULE PLANNING TIME
- PRIORITIZE
- KEEP A TIME LOG
- PLAN
- USE PLANNERS

- USE PLANNING SOFTWARE
- FILE EFFICIENTLY
- CONTROL APPOINTMENTS
- MANAGE YOUR WRITING

PERSONAL TIME-MANAGEMENT PLAN

CAN YOU FIND 4 EXTRA HOURS?

Time-Management Techniques You Might Employ	*Time Saved Per Day*

Total Time Found! _____

WHAT D'YA KNOW? (INDIVIDUAL VERSION)

In a Nutshell

Participants take a short quiz that measures their "motivational competencies"—basic skills that allow people to boost their motivation. A discussion follows in which people discuss ways of strengthening these competencies.

What It's For

Use this game if you want to: perform at your peak; test people's motivational skills.

Time

30 minutes.

What You'll Learn

To a great extent, we can control our own level of motivation. The skills we exercise to do so are called "motivational competencies," and such competencies can be measured and improved.

201

What You'll Need

Writing materials, along with copies of the handouts on pages 205 and 206.

What to Do

Distribute copies of the handout on page 205, answer questions people might have about the test, and have people complete it. This should take between 5 and 10 minutes. Then distribute copies of the form on page 206, and have people self-score the test. The latter will allow people to generate an overall score, as well as sub-scores in four key areas of motivational competency:

1) Manages environment
2) Manages thoughts
3) Sets goals
4) Maintains a healthful lifestyle

In addition to these four, mention four other competency areas (measured in the full version of the *Epstein Motivation Competencies Inventory for Individuals [EMCI-i]*, but not in the abridged version), as follows:

5) Manages consequences
6) Self-monitors
7) Builds skills
8) Manages stress

For further information about these competencies, see the chapter entitled "Motivation Basics" (page 3). To focus on managerial competencies rather than on individual competencies, see the next chapter in this book (page 207).

Lead a brief discussion about what the scores mean and about how participants might get additional training to sharpen their skills. (The games in this book can be used for this purpose.)

Discussion Questions

1. Where are your motivational competencies strong? Where can you use some improvement?
2. Were you surprised by the results of the quiz? How so?
3. What additional training would you like to have to improve your motivational competencies? How might this lead to better performance and a brighter outlook?

If You're Short on Time

Administer the test orally, having people record their answers on a blank sheet of paper, and then talk them through the scoring.

Tip!

The test included in this chapter is a shortened version of the *Epstein Motivation Competencies Inventory for Individuals*

(EMCI-i). The full, validated test can be obtained from InnoGen International (1-877-INNOGEN or www.innogen.com). It can be administered online or on a personal computer, and a version is also available at www.dreamlife.com.

The following chapter includes a shortened version of the managerial form of the test.

EPSTEIN MOTIVATION COMPETENCIES INVENTORY
for Individuals (EMCI-i) [Abridged]

Please use a pencil to fill in the bubble that best represents your reaction to each statement.

1. My work area is an ideal place in which to work. *Agree* ① ② ③ ④ ⑤ *Disagree*

2. I never picture a bright future for myself. *Agree* ① ② ③ ④ ⑤ *Disagree*

3. I work with difficult people. *Agree* ① ② ③ ④ ⑤ *Disagree*

4. The colors in my work area really energize me. *Agree* ① ② ③ ④ ⑤ *Disagree*

5. I think it's possible to look at anything in a positive way. *Agree* ① ② ③ ④ ⑤ *Disagree*

6. Food has no impact on mood. *Agree* ① ② ③ ④ ⑤ *Disagree*

7. I regularly set goals for myself. *Agree* ① ② ③ ④ ⑤ *Disagree*

8. It's impossible to look at everything in a positive way. *Agree* ① ② ③ ④ ⑤ *Disagree*

9. I exercise regularly. *Agree* ① ② ③ ④ ⑤ *Disagree*

10. I plan each day carefully. *Agree* ① ② ③ ④ ⑤ *Disagree*

11. I rarely feel well rested when I wake up in the morning. *Agree* ① ② ③ ④ ⑤ *Disagree*

12. I frequently visualize inspirational scenes. *Agree* ① ② ③ ④ ⑤ *Disagree*

13. My work area is poorly designed. *Agree* ① ② ③ ④ ⑤ *Disagree*

14. I have specific goals for my future. *Agree* ① ② ③ ④ ⑤ *Disagree*

15. I do aerobic exercise several times a week. *Agree* ① ② ③ ④ ⑤ *Disagree*

16. I really like the people with whom I work. *Agree* ① ② ③ ④ ⑤ *Disagree*

17. When I need a boost certain foods and drinks really help me. *Agree* ① ② ③ ④ ⑤ *Disagree*

18. Goal setting has no effect on performance. *Agree* ① ② ③ ④ ⑤ *Disagree*

19. I always get a good night's sleep. *Agree* ① ② ③ ④ ⑤ *Disagree*

20. I can look at anything in a positive way. *Agree* ① ② ③ ④ ⑤ *Disagree*

21. My work area is designed to help me perform at my peak. *Agree* ① ② ③ ④ ⑤ *Disagree*

22. I have no long-term goals. *Agree* ① ② ③ ④ ⑤ *Disagree*

23. Goal setting improves performance. *Agree* ① ② ③ ④ ⑤ *Disagree*

24. Daydreaming about a positive future is a waste of time. *Agree* ① ② ③ ④ ⑤ *Disagree*

205

Self-Scorer for EMCI-i [Abridged]

To score your test: Generate your <u>total score</u> by listing a <u>1</u> or a <u>0</u> in the blanks in the left-hand column below. Give yourself a <u>1</u> if you filled in a bubble in the shaded areas; otherwise give yourself a <u>0</u>. Count up the 1's and fill in your <u>total score</u> at the bottom of the column. The highest possible score is a <u>24</u>. If you scored lower than that, you can probably improve your motivational competencies. To focus on specific <u>competencies</u>, complete the four boxes below by circling item numbers for which you received a score of <u>1</u>. In each box, count the 1's, and fill in the blank with the total. If you scored below the maximum, you may need to strengthen your skills within that competency area.

1. ❶ ❷ ③ ④ ⑤___
2. ① ② ③ ❹ ❺___
3. ① ② ③ ❹ ❺___
4. ❶ ❷ ③ ④ ⑤___
5. ❶ ❷ ③ ④ ⑤___
6. ① ② ③ ❹ ❺___
7. ❶ ❷ ③ ④ ⑤___
8. ① ② ③ ❹ ❺___
9. ❶ ❷ ③ ④ ⑤___
10. ❶ ❷ ③ ④ ⑤___
11. ① ② ③ ❹ ❺___
12. ❶ ❷ ③ ④ ⑤___
13. ① ② ③ ❹ ❺___
14. ❶ ❷ ③ ④ ⑤___
15. ❶ ❷ ③ ④ ⑤___
16. ❶ ❷ ③ ④ ⑤___
17. ❶ ❷ ③ ④ ⑤___
18. ① ② ③ ❹ ❺___
19. ❶ ❷ ③ ④ ⑤___
20. ❶ ❷ ③ ④ ⑤___
21. ❶ ❷ ③ ④ ⑤___
22. ① ② ③ ❹ ❺___
23. ❶ ❷ ③ ④ ⑤___
24. ① ② ③ ❹ ❺___

TOTAL SCORE:_____/24

---

1) Manages environment. You create a workspace that helps to energize you, and you surround yourself with people who bring out your best.

| 1 | 3 | 4 | 13 | 16 | 21 | Total 1's: ____ / 6 |

---

2) Manages thoughts. You use visualization techniques, thought-restructuring techniques, and affirmations to keep yourself thinking positively.

| 2 | 5 | 8 | 12 | 20 | 24 | Total 1's: ____ / 6 |

---

3) Sets goals. You make both short-term and long-term goals, and you formulate plans for how to achieve those goals.

| 7 | 10 | 14 | 18 | 22 | 23 | Total 1's:____ / 6 |

---

4) Maintains a healthful lifestyle. You exercise regularly, get adequate sleep, and eat right in order to keep your energy high.

| 6 | 9 | 11 | 15 | 17 | 19 | Total 1's:____ / 6 |

WHAT D'YA KNOW? (MANAGERS VERSION)

In a Nutshell

Participants take a short quiz, designed for managers, supervisors, and teachers, which measures "motivational competencies"—basic skills that allow managers to motivate other people. A discussion follows in which people discuss ways of strengthening these competencies.

What It's For

Use this game if you want to: improve your managerial skills; help managers improve their managerial skills; test people's motivational skills.

Time

30 minutes.

What You'll Learn

We can measure and improve our ability to motivate others.

What You'll Need

Writing materials, along with copies of the handouts on pages 211 and 212.

What to Do

Distribute copies of the handout on page 211, answer questions people might have about the test, and have people complete it. This should take between 5 and 10 minutes. Then distribute copies of the form on page 212, and have people self-score the test. The latter will allow people to generate an overall score, as well as sub-scores in four key areas of motivational competency:

1) Manages rewards
2) Communicates effectively
3) Manages teams effectively
4) Manages environment

In addition to these four, mention six other competency areas (measured in the full version of the *Epstein Motivation Competencies Inventory for Managers [EMCI-m]*, but not in the abridged version), as follows:

5) Resolves conflicts
6) Matches skills with tasks
7) Allocates resources effectively
8) Trains and teaches
9) Challenges workers
10) Models high-energy behavior

For further information about these competencies, see the chapter entitled "Motivation Basics" (page 3). To focus on individual competencies rather than on managerial competencies, see the previous chapter in this book (page 201).

Lead a brief discussion about what the scores mean and about how participants might get additional training to sharpen their skills. The games in this book can be used for this purpose.

Discussion Questions

1. Where are your motivational competencies strong? Where can you use some improvement?
2. Were you surprised by the results of the quiz? How so?
3. What additional training would you like to have to improve your motivational competencies? How might this lead to better performance in motivating others?

If You're Short on Time

To speed things up, administer the test orally, having people record their answers on a blank sheet of paper, and then talk them through the scoring.

Tip!

The test included in this chapter is a shortened version of the *Epstein Motivation Competencies Inventory for Managers*

(EMCI-m). The full, validated test can be obtained from InnoGen International (1-877-INNOGEN or www.innogen.com). It can be administered online or on a personal computer, and a version is also available at www.dreamlife.com.

EPSTEIN MOTIVATION COMPETENCIES INVENTORY
for Managers (EMCI-m) [Abridged]

Please use a pencil to fill in the bubble that best represents your reaction to each statement.

1. Rewards have little value in maintaining good performance. *Agree* ① ② ③ ④ ⑤ *Disagree*

2. I welcome people's questions. *Agree* ① ② ③ ④ ⑤ *Disagree*

3. Office parties can be great motivators. *Agree* ① ② ③ ④ ⑤ *Disagree*

4. I try to communicate a clear vision of the future to employees. *Agree* ① ② ③ ④ ⑤ *Disagree*

5. When a team member is weak in some area, I try to ignore that. *Agree* ① ② ③ ④ ⑤ *Disagree*

6. I rarely ask employees to give me feedback on my ideas. *Agree* ① ② ③ ④ ⑤ *Disagree*

7. Instructions motivate people better than rewards do. *Agree* ① ② ③ ④ ⑤ *Disagree*

8. I use color to boost productivity throughout the workplace. *Agree* ① ② ③ ④ ⑤ *Disagree*

9. How well my employees get along is not my business. *Agree* ① ② ③ ④ ⑤ *Disagree*

10. It's not clear how to transform a group into a team. *Agree* ① ② ③ ④ ⑤ *Disagree*

11. I try to inspire my team with clear visions and goals. *Agree* ① ② ③ ④ ⑤ *Disagree*

12. I often reward excellence among my employees. *Agree* ① ② ③ ④ ⑤ *Disagree*

13. I use ergonomic principles to equip my workspace. *Agree* ① ② ③ ④ ⑤ *Disagree*

14. Everyone on a team is capable of making similar contributions. *Agree* ① ② ③ ④ ⑤ *Disagree*

15. I always acknowledge contributions of employees. *Agree* ① ② ③ ④ ⑤ *Disagree*

16. Irritating sounds can damage motivation. *Agree* ① ② ③ ④ ⑤ *Disagree*

17. People generally find the same things rewarding. *Agree* ① ② ③ ④ ⑤ *Disagree*

18. Within a team, cooperation is more important than competition. *Agree* ① ② ③ ④ ⑤ *Disagree*

19. I try to involve employees in many aspects of decision making. *Agree* ① ② ③ ④ ⑤ *Disagree*

20. I regularly help my team to reach consensus on key issues. *Agree* ① ② ③ ④ ⑤ *Disagree*

21. Lighting has little effect on performance. *Agree* ① ② ③ ④ ⑤ *Disagree*

22. I often solicit ideas from my employees. *Agree* ① ② ③ ④ ⑤ *Disagree*

23. Rewards must be distributed fairly for them to be effective. *Agree* ① ② ③ ④ ⑤ *Disagree*

24. I try to inspire my employees to perform well. *Agree* ① ② ③ ④ ⑤ *Disagree*

211

Self-Scorer for EMCI-m [Abridged]

To score your test: *Generate your <u>total score</u> by listing a <u>1</u> or a <u>0</u> in the blanks in the left-hand column below. Give yourself a <u>1</u> if you filled in a bubble in the shaded areas; otherwise give yourself a <u>0</u>. Count up the 1's and fill in your <u>total score</u> at the bottom of the column. The highest possible score is a <u>24</u> If you scored lower than that, you can probably improve your ability to motivate people. To focus on specific <u>competencies</u>, complete the four boxes below by circling item numbers for which you received a score of <u>1</u>. In each box, count the 1's, and fill in the blank with the total. If you scored below the maximum, you may need to strengthen your skills within that competency area.*

1. ① ② ③ **④ ⑤** ___
2. **① ②** ③ ④ ⑤ ___
3. **① ②** ③ ④ ⑤ ___
4. **① ②** ③ ④ ⑤ ___
5. ① ② ③ **④ ⑤** ___
6. ① ② ③ **④ ⑤** ___
7. ① ② ③ **④ ⑤** ___
8. **① ②** ③ ④ ⑤ ___
9. ① ② ③ **④ ⑤** ___
10. ① ② ③ **④ ⑤** ___
11. **① ②** ③ ④ ⑤ ___
12. **① ②** ③ ④ ⑤ ___
13. **① ②** ③ ④ ⑤ ___
14. ① ② ③ **④ ⑤** ___
15. **① ②** ③ ④ ⑤ ___
16. **① ②** ③ ④ ⑤ ___
17. ① ② ③ **④ ⑤** ___
18. **① ②** ③ ④ ⑤ ___
19. **① ②** ③ ④ ⑤ ___
20. **① ②** ③ ④ ⑤ ___
21. ① ② ③ **④ ⑤** ___
22. **① ②** ③ ④ ⑤ ___
23. **① ②** ③ ④ ⑤ ___
24. **① ②** ③ ④ ⑤ ___

TOTAL SCORE: _____ /24

1) Manages rewards. You provide positive and constructive feedback, recognize accomplishment, and reward good performance.

| 1 | 7 | 12 | 15 | 17 | 23 | *Total 1's: ____ / 6* |

2) Communicates effectively. You solicit ideas and feedback, present a clear vision of the future, and seek to inform, educate, and inspire.

| 2 | 4 | 6 | 19 | 22 | 24 | *Total 1's: ____ / 6* |

3) Manages teams effectively. You compose teams wisely and help them to function smoothly and optimally.

| 5 | 10 | 11 | 14 | 18 | 20 | *Total 1's: ____ / 6* |

4) Manages environment. You create and maintain an attractive, functional workspace and encourage healthy relationships.

| 3 | 8 | 9 | 13 | 16 | 21 | *Total 1's: ____ / 6* |

WORKPLACE CHALLENGE

In a Nutshell

Participants work in teams to develop specific methods for improving motivation in their own workplace environments.

What It's For

Use this game if you want to: motivate your staff members to perform at their peak; help managers to improve their managerial skills; motivate chronically underperforming employees; motivate people in a large organization; design a motivating environment.

Time

20–30 minutes.

What You'll Learn

You can apply what you've learned about motivation to suit your specific work situation.

What You'll Need

Writing materials for each participant.

What to Do

Divide the group into small teams, and have the teams spend about 15 minutes compiling lists of methods that might enhance motivation in their workplaces. If you like, use the "shifting" technique to enhance the creativity of your teams: Have people work together for a few minutes, then have them work alone for a few minutes, then have them shift back into the group (see "The Shifting Game" in *The Big Book of Creativity Games* for more information about shifting).

After the teams are done, have representatives of different teams share their results with the group, and lead a discussion about practical ways of improving workplace motivation. If your resources allow, collect the lists, compile them into a master list, and distribute it (by email, perhaps) to all participants.

Discussion Questions

1. Describe some specific ways in which your particular organization might increase individual motivation.
2. Describe some specific ways in which your organization might train and motivate managers to motivate other people more effectively.

3. Which of your proposals are most feasible? Which are least feasible? Why?
4. What's a reasonable timetable for increasing motivation in your workplace?
5. What are the main concepts (from this book or elsewhere) that you're relying on to try to boost motivation in your workplace?
6. How optimistic are you that these changes can be made? Please explain.

THE YES! GAME

In a Nutshell

Participants use a high-energy "shaping" procedure to get the group leader to do something unusual.

What It's For

Use this game if you want to: motivate your staff members to perform at their peak; improve your managerial skills; spark peak team performance; motivate people in a large organization; motivate salespeople.

Time

20 minutes.

What You'll Learn

Reinforcement is a powerful tool for motivating and teaching!

What You'll Need

No special materials or supplies are needed.

What to Do

Explain to the participants that you're going to leave the room briefly. Tell them that while you're out of the room, they'll need to pick something fairly simple but unusual for you to do when you return (like removing your tie or doing the funky chicken). Explain that when you enter the room, they can't *tell you* or *show you* what you're supposed to do. All they can do is shout "Yes!"—preferably, in unison.

Explain that, at first, they should shout "Yes!" whenever they see you doing anything that's even vaguely related to the target behavior. For example, if they're trying to get you to touch your ear, they should shout "Yes!" when you move your hand even slightly upward. Then they should shout "Yes" when, over time, they see closer and closer approximations to the target behavior—for example, hand movements closer and closer to your ear. Remind the group that there's *no* saying *"No."* Have everyone practice the shout a few times to get them warmed up.

Now pick a volunteer to help the group select the target behavior, and tell the volunteer that he or she should bring you back into the room after the group has made its selection. Leave the room. After a few minutes, the volunteer will retrieve you, and you should have some fun while the group "shapes" your behavior with shouts of "Yes!"

Afterward, explain that this game demonstrates how positive reinforcement, used in a shaping procedure, can get someone to behave in new ways. More generally, it also shows the power that reinforcement has to change behavior.

Discussion Questions

1. How long did it take you to "shape" the first target behavior? How long did you expect to take?
2. The "Yes!" was functioning in this exercise as a positive reinforcer. What kind of behavior can you strengthen with positive reinforcers? Is there any behavior you can't strengthen with positive reinforcers?
3. What are some advantages of using positive reinforcement to change behavior? Are there any disadvantages? If so, what are they?
4. Describe some situations in which positive reinforcement is used wisely in your work or home environments? How could it be used in additional ways?

If You Have More Time

Repeat the procedure using volunteers as subjects. Have the group select an unusual new target behavior each time. If you like, have someone time each performance. How long does it take—using positive reinforcement alone!—to get someone to perform an unusual behavior? (Typically, it will only take a minute or two!)

Tip!

The target behaviors can be highly unusual, but they should also be relatively simple, by which we mean that the target behaviors should not involve a long sequence of actions. Sequences can be taught by shaping, but the procedure is more complex than the one specified in this chapter. Also, we'd recommend that you avoid trying to get the subject to say or write something. Language can be shaped (see "The Tiny Little Nod Game," page 193), but, again, the procedure is different from the one described here.

INDEX

222

ABOUT THE AUTHORS

One of the world's leading experts on human behavior, ROBERT EPSTEIN is Editor-in-Chief of *Psychology Today* magazine and host of the magazine's Internet-based radio program (accessible at www.psychtoday.com). Dr. Epstein is also University Research Professor at United States International University in San Diego, Chairman and CEO of InnoGen International, and the founder and Director Emeritus of the Cambridge Center for Behavioral Studies in Massachusetts. He received his Ph.D. in psychology in 1981 from Harvard University. He is the developer of Generativity Theory, a scientific theory of the creative process, and a contributor to the *Encyclopedia of Creativity*. His research on creativity and problem solving has been reported in *Time* magazine, the *New York Times*, and *Discover*, as well as on national and international radio and television. Epstein's recent books include *The Big Book of Creativity Games* (McGraw-Hill), *The Big Book of Stress-Relief Games* (McGraw-Hill), *Stress-Management and Relaxation Activities for Trainers* (McGraw-Hill), *The New Psychology Today Reader* (Kendall/Hunt), *Creativity Games for Trainers* (McGraw-Hill), *Cognition, Creativity, and Behavior: Selected Essays* (Praeger), *Pure Fitness: Body Meets Mind* (Masters Press, with Lori "Ice" Fetrick of "The American Gladiators"), *Self-Help Without the Hype* (Performance Management Publications), and *Irrelativity* (Astrion). He is also the editor of two books of writings by the eminent psychologist, B. F. Skinner, with whom Epstein collaborated at Harvard. He has served on the faculties of Boston University, the University of Massachusetts at Amherst, the University of California San Diego, and other universities. He served as Professor of Psychology and Chair of the Department of Psychology at National University and was also appointed Research Professor there. He is also Adjunct Professor of Psychology at San Diego State University. Dr. Epstein directed the Loebner Prize Competition in Artificial Intelligence for five years and has done consulting and training for businesses and mental health programs for more than fifteen years. He has been a commentator for NPR's "Marketplace" and the Voice of America, and his popular writings have appeared in *Reader's Digest*, *The Washington Post*, *Psychology Today*, *Good Housekeeping, Parenting*, and other magazines and newspapers. Dr. Epstein can be reached by email at repstein@post.harvard.edu. JESSICA ROGERS is a freelance writer, an Editorial Intern for *Psychology Today* magazine, and a student at the University of California Berkeley.